Lysander

KEY
Books

HISTORIC MILITARY AIRCRAFT SERIES, VOLUME 20

Contents page image: The first prototype Westland Lysander, K6127, pictured in August 1938. (Via Martyn Chorlton)

Published by Key Books
An imprint of Key Publishing Ltd
PO Box 100
Stamford
Lincs PE9 1XQ

www.keypublishing.com

Original edition published as *Aeroplane Icons: Lysander*
© 2013, edited by Martyn Chorlton

This edition © 2022

ISBN 978 1 80282 459 9

Typeset by SJmagic DESIGN SERVICES, India.

Contents

A Miracle of Flappery and Slattery

T he Westland Lysander is one of Britain's, if not the world's, most easily identifiable aircraft, and during its heyday the plane spotter's mantra was simply divided into two categories: 'aircraft and Lysanders'.

Originally designed for army co-operation duties, the Lysander was actually a failure in this role, through no fault of the aircraft or its outstanding design, which met the original specification A.39/34. Instead, the blame lay with senior Air Staff, who were so focused on the strategic concepts of air warfare, they completely overlooked the importance of aerial liaison and support with ground forces; as a result, only four army co-operation squadrons were sent to France with the British Expeditionary Force (BEF) in 1939. Compare this to 1918, when the RAF was formed; the tasking allotted to the Royal Flying Corps (RFC) was embraced, and at least 20 squadrons undertook army co-operation – ironically over the very same terrain, although the second Great War would obviously not be as

Lined up at Baldonnel not long after they were delivered are all six of the Irish Air Corps (IAC) Westland Lysander Mk IIs. The last IAC example was retired in April 1947. (Via Martyn Chorlton)

static as the first. Another analogy with World War One was that the Lysander was poorly armed in comparison to the biplanes over the trenches that enjoyed the same calibre weapons, generally had more of them and, compared to the enclosed cockpits of the 'Lizzie', had a better field of fire.

The Lysander's career as an army co-operation aircraft was short, but it would be in other roles the type was destined to make a real name for itself. A Lysander would have been a welcome sight to a downed pilot in the sea during the early stages of World War Two, and, in much the same way, an agent seeking to return to England in the middle of the night, likewise, would have embraced the 'Lizzie'. The Lysander was also heavily used at air gunnery schools, and a multitude of target-towing flights gave fledgling fighter pilots their first taste of firing live rounds at a moving target.

The Lysander was one of the world's first Short Take-off and Landing (STOL) aircraft, thanks to the wonder of flaps and slats designed into a wing of unique design. Harald Penrose took great pleasure in demonstrating the Lysander's flying ability to the general public during pre-war airshows. The Lysander never ceases to amaze those who see it; its sheer size alone defies its flying qualities, and its ungainly appearance belies the aircraft's true versatility. The Lysander is, and will always be, one of the world's great iconic flying machines.

A show of force by a group of army co-operation Lysanders, purely for the benefit of the press from a Wiltshire airfield before the beginning of World War Two. The stark reality of war and the pace of the Battle of France rendered the type obsolete overnight for its intended role. (*Aeroplane*)

Chapter 1

Replacing the Audax

Advancing army co-operation

A contemporary of the Hurricane and Spitfire fighters and the Blenheim and Whitley bombers, the Westland Lysander was the RAF's first monoplane army co-operation aircraft. It was one of many new aircraft that were brought into service as part of the RAF Expansion Scheme, which was prompted by the rise and increasing threat of Germany's Third Reich. The Lysander's eventual selection followed submissions from three other aircraft manufacturers, Hawker, Bristol and Avro (not pursued beyond preliminary drawings), to specification A.39/34 (issued in April 1935) for a two-seat army co-operation aircraft.

Hawker was the first to present its ideas for A.39/34, and it was clearly in the strongest position of all the manufacturers, thanks to its own Hawker Audax, which was the existing army co-operation aircraft of choice. Ironically, the Audax was produced under contract by a number of manufacturers, including Yeovil-based Westland. Even though the Hawker design was not accepted by the Air Ministry, Westland still benefitted, as an order was placed for the Napier Dagger-powered Hector, and its entire production of 179 aircraft was sub-contracted to the Yeovil-based manufacturer.

The only other remotely serious contender for A.39/34 was Bristol with its Type 148, of which two prototypes were ordered, K6551 and K6552, the first not flying until 15 October 1937 (16 months after the Lysander). Powered by a Bristol Mercury IX engine, the Type 148 had an impressive speed range of 62–225mph, which was ideal for co-operation work, but neither figure reached those written in the specification. One of the many requirements for such an aircraft was the ability to loiter and/or fly very slowly to pick-up messages and then deliver them at speed. All seemed to be going well for Bristol until it came to the specification's configuration demands. The Type 148 was a low-wing design, and, as the aircraft would have to be capable of landing on very rough airfields or temporary strips, a wing tip may become fouled and damaged because of the uneven surface. More importantly, the 275sq ft wing obstructed a large amount of the ground, which is what the crew were supposed to be observing! It was obvious from a very early stage that there was going to be only one serious contender in this competition.

Developed from the highly successful Hawker Hart light bomber, the Audax was specifically designed for the army co-operation role. First flown in 1931, more than 700 were built, 625 of them serving the RAF alone between 1932 and 1937. (Via Martyn Chorlton)

Designed to the same A.39/34 specification as the Lysander, the Bristol Type 148 did not undertake its maiden flight until 16 months after the 'Lizzie'. (Via Martyn Chorlton)

The Westland P.8

Westland had been doing its homework regarding exactly what the role of army co-operation involved before the company submitted its proposal for A.39/34. To help achieve this, it obtained permission from the Air Ministry to view how the role of army co-operation was conducted in the field. Within days, the entire Westland design team found themselves at No.1 School of Army Co-operation at Old Sarum near Salisbury, which had been training both army and RAF personnel in Wiltshire since 1920.

The Westland A.39/34 (P.8) K6127, fitted with a two-blade, fixed-pitch Watts propeller, was only used for taxiing trials. The aircraft is shown before the final aluminium doping was applied and the undercarriage spatted. (Via Martyn Chorlton)

The school was tasked with training, on average, 20 officers at a time on a 12-week course. The itinerary included tutorials on a host of subjects, including artillery reconnaissance, photography, signalling and general military organisation. Originally, and certainly towards the tail end of World War One, much of this tasking was carried out by the observer, but, by the mid-to-late 1930s, this had been transferred to the pilot. The observer was now responsible for the defence of the aircraft, and this was an important factor that influenced how the team would design the cockpit.

The ability to fly at a very slow speed and still maintain full control was also in the forefront of the designer's mind. The autogyro was under serious consideration for army co-operation duties at the time, and Westland knew that it would have to incorporate the ability to achieve a STOL capability. By early 1935, the project, under the Westland designation of P.8, was born.

Ingenuity and potential

In 1935, there was a shake-up amongst the hierarchy of Westland Aircraft, which saw one of the founding members of the company, Sir Ernest Petter, hand the job of technical director to his son, William Edward Willoughby 'Teddy' Petter. Petter joined the company in 1929 as a graduate apprentice, and his rapid rise to technical director was not received well by many of the senior management; as a result several left for pastures new.

Under 'Teddy' Petter was chief designer Arthur Davenport, who first joined Petters Ltd, an engineering company also based in Yeovil, in 1912. When Westland was founded in 1915,

Harald Penrose demonstrates the short-field ability of the prototype Lysander, K6127. (Via Martyn Chorlton)

Davenport transferred to the new aircraft division, where he had remained ever since. Westland's forward-thinking design approach also included input from the company's chief test pilot, Harald Penrose, who would be ultimately responsible for the P.8's early flight testing. By mid-1935, an order for two P.8 prototypes was placed and allocated the RAF serials K6127 and K6128, both to be powered by a Bristol Mercury engine.

By early June 1936, the first aircraft, K6127, was complete. On 10 June, Harald Penrose began taxiing trials at Yeovil, and five days later the aircraft took to the air for the first time.

Hard-working prototypes

Following successful manufacturers' trials, K6127 was delivered to the Aeroplane & Armament Experimental Establishment (A&AEE), Martlesham Heath, on 26 November 1936, for performance and handling trials. Once these were complete, the aircraft was passed on to the Royal Aircraft Establishment (RAE) at Farnborough, before appearing in front of the general public for the first time at Hendon on 27 June, displaying 'New Types No.6' on the fuselage.

After further comings and goings between Farnborough and Yeovil, K6127 was fitted with a Mercury XII engine and, by June 1938, was back at the RAE for aerodynamic testing. Further performance trials were conducted at the A&AEE before the busy aircraft returned to Yeovil for almost two years.

From its maiden flight on 15 June 1936 right up until its withdrawal from use in early 1943, the prototype Lysander, K6127, was a hard-working machine. Modified and restored to its original configuration on numerous occasions, the aircraft was not struck off charge (SOC) from 9 Maintenance Unit (MU) at Cosford until June 1944. (Via Martyn Chorlton)

First flown on 11 December 1936, the second prototype Lysander, K6128, did not enjoy the long and varied career of its predecessor. (Via Martyn Chorlton)

K6127 was brought out of its semi-retirement for 20mm gun trials at the A&AEE in July 1940 and during August and September found itself on operational strength for the first and only time with 110 Squadron, Royal Canadian Air Force. By late 1940, the aircraft was back at Yeovil in preparation for a unique and extensive modification.

The Westland design team came up with a proposal for an aircraft for anti-invasion operations, specifically for strafing enemy ground forces. The solution was to fit a Boulton Paul four-gun turret into the end of the fuselage in the position once occupied by the tail, and replace the flying surfaces with a large span tailplane with twin fins and rudders at its extremities. The tailplane was so large it was effectively a second wing, a Delanne type, which increased the total wing area from 260–392sq ft. The fuselage was shortened by 4ft 9in, but, despite the dramatic change in appearance from the original P.8, Penrose stated that the aircraft handled very well, and tests at the A&AEE in October 1941 endorsed this. This aircraft has been retrospectively referred to by many names; the most accurate and most likely to have been adopted by Westland was the P.12 Wendover.

Returned to its original configuration, K6127 was modified again in 1942 for trials with castoring wheels and caterpillar tracks; both in an effort to improve the type's short strip and rough ground capability. By January 1943, the aircraft was placed in storage with 9 Maintenance Unit (MU) at Cosford, and remained there until it was struck off charge (SOC) on 13 June 1944.

The second prototype, K6128, first flew on 11 December 1936. The aircraft was delivered to the A&AEE, for the first time, on 1 April 1937, returning a few days later to Yeovil for fitment of a Mercury XII engine. Further performance, sound-proofing and tropical trials continued with the A&AEE through to early 1938, when it was despatched to Aboukir for 'in theatre' tropical trials with 31 Squadron. By May 1939, the aircraft began a tour of RAF units for service trials, including 20, 5 and 28 squadrons before being downgraded as a ground instructional airframe on 8 July 1940. Its fate beyond this date is unknown, but it would have done well to have survived as long as its predecessor.

Orders off the board

The Westland P.8 had clearly impressed the Air Ministry to such an extent that the first production run for 66 Mercury XII-powered aircraft (L4673 to L4738), under Contract No. 555425/36 was placed before the prototype had actually flown. A further order for another 78 Perseus XII-powered machines (L4739 to L4816) under the same contract was also placed before the second prototype had flown in December 1936.

The second production Lysander Mk I, L4674, was built by Westland at Yeovil under contract 555425/36. The aircraft is being taxied by a hatted Harald Penrose, very close to an appreciative audience. (Via Martyn Chorlton)

It was only once the first production order was placed that the aircraft was officially named the Lysander, following a long tradition of naming army co-operation (AC) machines with classical names. Lysander was the son of a Spartan Admiral, Aristocritus, who was one of the most powerful men in Greece in approximately 400 BC.

The first production Westland Lysander Mk I, L4673, left the Yeovil production line on 15 May 1938 before being passed on to the A&AEE for type testing. The second machine, L4674, was retained by Westland for tests with a Perseus XII engine, which would ultimately be installed in the Lysander Mk II for the second production order. L4675 was fitted with dual controls for the Central Flying School (CFS) at Upavon after a misunderstanding – the school actually required a standard production aircraft for the writing of handling notes; L4676 was supplied instead. Therefore, L4675 became the first Lysander to enter squadron service.

Into service

It was 4 Squadron at Odiham that was earmarked to be the first recipient of the Lysander; however, the unit was committed to taking part in a large mobilisation exercise and would have to fly its Hectors for a few months longer. 16 Squadron, under the command of Sqn Ldr T. Humble at Old Sarum, a unit that had been flying the Audax since December 1933, was chosen instead, receiving its first aircraft from late May 1938, with the bulk of them being on strength during June. 16 Squadron was an obvious second choice because the School of Army Co-operation was also based at Old Sarum, and 16 Squadron's pilots were regularly seconded to provide instruction for the students of the school.

Of the first batch of production Lysanders, 14 were issued to 16 Squadron and a further nine were allocated to the School of Army Co-operation. 2 (AC) Squadron followed in July 1938 at Hawkinge under the command of Sqn Ldr A. J. W. Geddes, who, like the majority of army co-operation commanding officers, was seconded to the RAF from the Royal Artillery, where he had served as a captain. 4 Squadron, under the command of Sqn Ldr G. P. Charles, was next in December, and then 13 (AC) Squadron also at Odiham, under the command of Sqn Ldr S. C. H. Gray, gave up its Hectors in favour of the Lysander from 23 January 1939. Lysanders were also issued to 26 Squadron at Catterick

16 Squadron, the first RAF unit to receive the Lysander, shows off three of its aircraft during a press photo call in 1939. The unit operated the type from May 1938 through to July 1942. (*Aeroplane*)

in place of their old Hectors in February 1939, and the final unit in Britain to receive the type before the outbreak of World War Two was 614 (County of Glamorgan) Squadron in July at Pengam Moors. The one exception to the home-based units was 208 (AC) Squadron at Heliopolis, Egypt, which began to receive the Lysander Mk I and Mk II from January 1939.

K6127 displays Experimental Park number '6' prior to its public appearance at Hendon in 1936. (Via Martyn Chorlton)

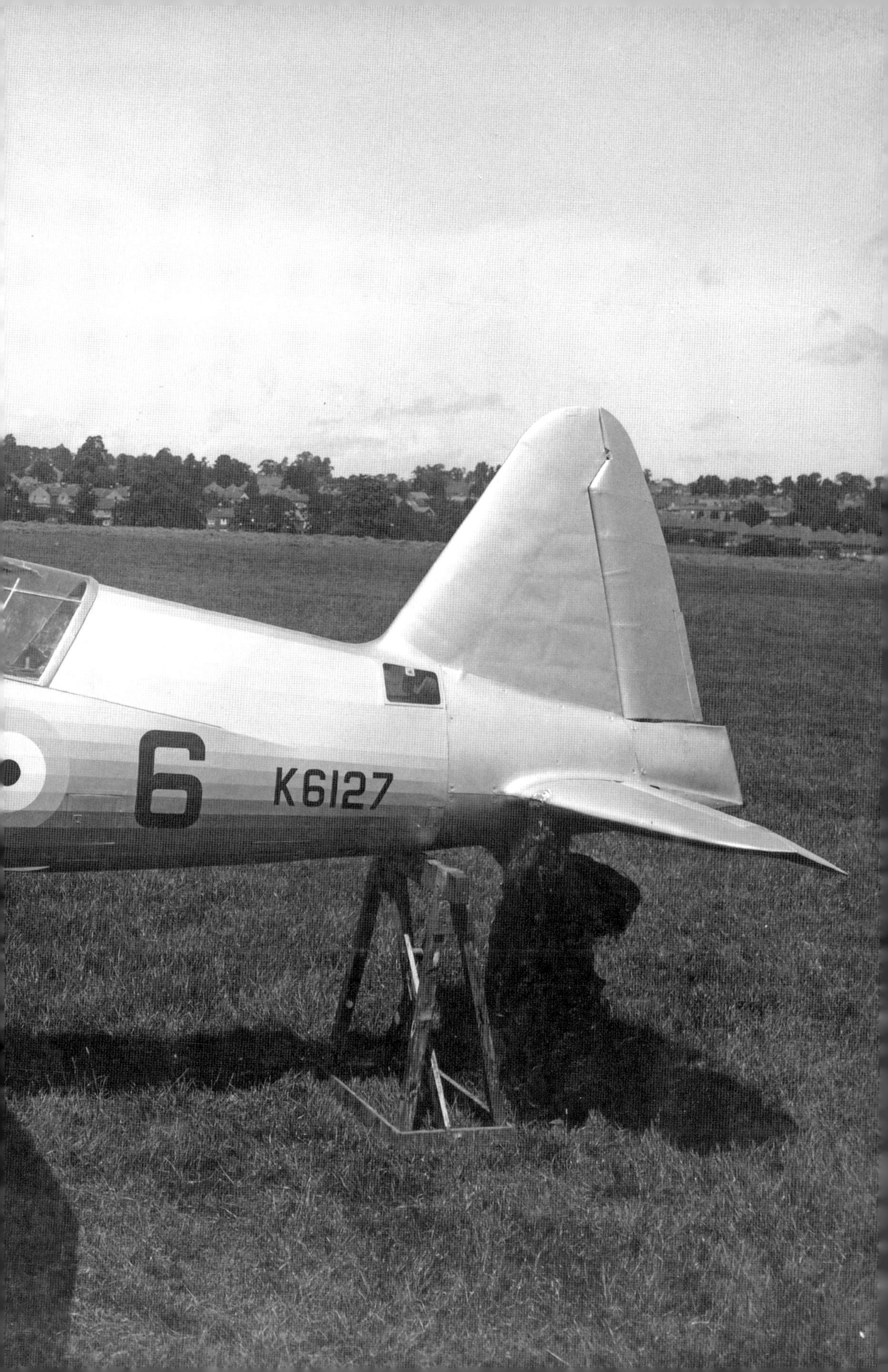
6
K6127

Chapter 2

First in Service

Return to France

4 Squadron was no stranger to operating in France, having served there from August 1914 to the end of 1918 in the previous world conflict. During World War Two, although very few of this new generation of officers and airmen would realise it, they returned to the same skies to fight a completely different kind of war.

Under the control of 50 (Army Co-operation) Wing, which was part of the Air Component of the BEF, the squadron left its Odiham home, arriving at Mons-en-Chaussée via Southampton and Cherbourg on 24 September 1939. The squadron's Westland Lysander Mk IIs, which it had been operating since December 1938, arrived later in the day to find a chaotic and cramped airfield.

Lysander Mk II, L4742, during a pre-war army co-operation exercise using its long message pick-up hook. The aircraft was lost on 14 May 1940 when it was presumed to have been shot down by Oblt Kupka in a Bf 109 of 9/JG3. The 'Lizzie' was brought down over Gembloux and its crew, Fg Off Terence C. Clarke and AC 1 William S. Rodulson, were killed. (*Flight* via *Aeroplane*)

Located 20 miles east of Amiens, Mons-en-Chaussée was the temporary home of virtually all of the Air Component, and 4 Squadron's personnel found themselves scattered in a variety of buildings in the local village, initially without blankets or rations because their supporting vehicles had become lost after leaving Cherbourg.

Under the temporary command of Sqn Ldr P. L. Donkin, and later Sqn Ldr Maffett, 4 Squadron wasted no time in flying as many familiarisation sorties as possible. Their operational area was up to and along the Belgian border down to the Maginot Line, and every opportunity was also taken to photograph as much of the landscape as possible. It was not long before the local area became very familiar, but this did not stop the occasional accidental foray into Belgian airspace, which would always result in a few rounds of flak to remind the aircrew where they were.

On 3 October 1939, operations became easier with a short move to Monchy-Lagache, ten miles west of Saint-Quentin. A false sense of security now descended upon the squadron, bolstered by sightseeing trips to the Maginot Line, which gave the impression of being impregnable. The 'Phoney War' was now in full swing, and the only enemy seemed to be boredom, which was staved off by regular parades and kit inspections. One consolation was an increase in sports afternoons.

The squadron had 12 Lysanders on strength at this time, divided into two flights. To vary and increase the operational coverage of the unit, a permanent detachment was established at Ronchin on the outskirts of Lille, less than ten miles from the Belgian border. Each flight took turns in operating from Ronchin on a weekly basis. This was a popular duty thanks to the high standard of the local bar, which would provide transport by tram back to the accommodation.

Operations by the squadron during the winter were almost non-existent, with both Monchy and Ronchin being reduced to a quagmire. Unbeknown to the BEF, it was this same weather that curtailed Hitler's offensive into France.

All smiles in this pre-war group photo of pilots (both RAF and Army) of 4 Squadron at RAF Odiham in early 1939. (4 Squadron records)

**4 SQUADRON COMMANDING OFFICERS,
OCTOBER 1938 TO APRIL 1942**

Sqn Ldr G. P. Charles	6 August 1939
Sqn Ldr P. L. Donkin	7 September 1940
Wg Cdr G. P. Charles	11 September 1940
Sqn Ldr Maffett	29 October 1940
Wg Cdr P. H. R. Saunders	9 December 1940
Wg Cdr G. P. Charles	12 February 1941

The 'Phoney War' comes to an end

Now under the command of newly promoted Wg Cdr G. P. Charles, OBE, 4 Squadron was expanded to 18 aircraft from March 1940, enabling the formation of 'C' Flight. All Lysander squadrons in France at the time were also increased in strength, making a total of 90 aircraft available. The average serviceability was a healthy 82 per cent, which meant that at least 74 Lysanders were on hand for daily operations in support of the BEF. With a larger number of aircraft, 4 Squadron operations continued through the spring, with almost daily sorties to local ranges to hone their bombing and air to ground strafing skills. However, the 'phoney' war was approaching its conclusion, and 'rumour control' was rife with news of the advancing Germans.

The realisation that the party in France was over came on 10 May 1940, when the Germans began their attack along the Dutch and Belgian borders, sweeping their weak armies aside and pushing on towards France. The attack started early for 4 Squadron with an He 111 spotted at 0403hrs flying low over the village of Monchy-Lagache without dropping a bomb. The squadron was immediately mobilised, with 'B' Flight moving to a satellite airfield at Crox Moligneaux, while 'A' Flight and a large proportion of ground personnel moved to Ronchin. In the afternoon, at least half a dozen He 111s flew over Monchy-Lagache, one of them was losing height. They were greeted with intense anti-aircraft fire from Royal Artillery 210 Battery, which shot one down in flames and caused a second to make a forced landing.

Only months earlier, flying over Belgium was strictly prohibited, but now its forces were desperately fighting a superior German force, and the BEF, along with 4 Squadron, pushed forward towards them. Several sorties were flown on 10 May; 4 Squadron was tasked with reconnaissance, photographic and contact patrols over positions that were at least four hours ahead of the Allied ground troops.

To operate even more effectively, 4 Squadron needed an Advanced Landing Ground (ALG) deep in Belgium. After quickly surveying several known landing grounds, Wg Cdr Charles opted for a new site located at Aspelaere, ten miles west of Brussels. It would require some work to prepare it, and a company of Royal Engineers was sent to the site, which it was hoped would be ready in just a few days. In the meantime, operations continued from Ronchin although the aircraft returned to Monchy-Lagache in the evening, reducing the chances of losing a batch of Lysanders in a single enemy raid.

By 13 May, 2 Corps was dug in along the River Dyle, and 4 Squadron was above reporting on enemy troop positions. First contact with the enemy was achieved by Plt Off B. Malins and LAC 'Ginger' Drew, who were lucky to make it back to Ronchin being attacked by several German anti-aircraft guns. The Luftwaffe was also operating in numbers, and at least one 4 Squadron Lysander was attacked by no fewer than nine Bf 109s but managed to escape, albeit with 32 holes

FRANCE AND LOW COUNTRIES 1939~1940

THE GREAT WHITE CHIEF

Wing Commander
Charles
4 Sqdy.

Nicknamed the 'Big White Chief' in this caricature, this is Wg Cdr G. P. Charles, who was Officer Commanding 4 Squadron on three separate occasions, including the period of the Battle of France. (4 Squadron records)

for the experience. As the Lysanders encountered ever-increasing numbers of enemy fighters, it was only a matter of time before the first casualty was recorded: Fg Off P. W. Vaughan and his air gunner AC E. Mold. After flying over enemy positions on the banks of the Gete river, the Lysander was shot down by a Bf 109 flown by Lt H. Braxator of 2./JG1 and crashed between Outgaarden and Goetsenhoven.

Advancing towards the enemy

'B' Flight was moved forward to the now-completed Aspelaere at midday on 14 May. It was literally only fit for Lysander operations, taking nothing away from the excellent hard work of the sappers in getting it ready so quickly. Unfortunately, 4 Squadron's arrival did not go that smoothly, as another Lysander was needlessly written off while attempting to land – Plt Off Hankey and Sgt Lewis survived the accident, but P1711 would never fly again. Two more Lysanders would also be lost before the day was out, this time to enemy fighters. Fg Off T. C. Clarke and AC W. S. Rodulson are believed to have fallen victim to the guns of Oblt Kupka's Bf 109 of 9./JG3. Neither survived after their aircraft, L4742, crashed into the village of Campagne du Reck. The same fate befell Plt Off D. M. Barbour and Cpl R. H. Waters in Lysander II L4745; sadly, they were never found. By the end of 14 May, 4 Squadron was down to 11 serviceable aircraft, and its loss rate was already unsustainable.

The following day, it was decided that the entire squadron would move forward to Ronchin while still maintaining detachments at Aspelaere and Clairmarais. By midday on 16 May, the move was complete, with 'B' Flight now operating from the ALG at Aspelaere. 'B' Flight now found itself covering the massed withdrawal of 2 Corp, and it was another frantic day of action for 4 Squadron. Plt Off Langley and his air gunner, LAC J. H. Gillham, came under sustained attack by six Bf 110s while flying an observation sortie near Louvain. Despite the overwhelming odds, Gillham claimed to have shot down one of the twin-engined fighters before their Lysander, L4814, force-landed near Lille. Another aircraft, P9064, flown by Fg Off E. E. Wood and air gunner Cpl J. Bower, also failed to return from a tactical reconnaissance sortie. Wood was killed, while Bower is believed to have survived.

Despite its anonymity, a Lysander was seen landing at Aspelaere on 17 May by a Luftwaffe spotter aircraft, and by 1600hrs the ALG was under attack by several Ju 87s, although luckily most of their bombs fell south of the small airfield. No significant damage was caused, but it was clear that there was no place for 4 Squadron to hide, and by now the BEF was also on the back foot as the Germans had already broken through the French lines. The morale of the squadron was under great strain, and this was only marginally lifted when five new Lysanders were collected from Glisy to help stem the tide of the squadron's losses.

It was clear that the ALG was under threat of being overrun by the enemy, and in the early hours of 18 May only Wg Cdr Charles and a couple of officers remained, while the remnants of 'B' Flight returned to Ronchin. 'A' Flight was now dispersed to another site at Lille Marcq, while 'C' Flight carried out the bulk of the day's operations. This included conducting reconnaissance along the River Dendre to monitor the advance of the enemy towards Brussels. It was on one of these sorties that Fg Off E. C. Ford and Fg Off K. W. Graham in N1263 came under attack by several Bf 109s. The Lysander stood no chance, falling to the guns of Oblt Rempel and Uffz Wischnewski of 6./JG2, southeast of Brussels. Neither of the airmen survived.

Needless losses

What seems like a great waste of both aircrew and aircraft occurred on 19 May, when a pair of Lysanders of 'A' Flight were conducting practice landings at Lille Marcq. It seems remarkable that a task like this would be undertaken in such a hostile environment; the choice of location resulted in four aircrew dead and two more aircraft destroyed. A large formation of Bf 109s from both 2 and 3(J)/LG2 pounced on the unsuspecting Lysanders, quickly dispatching both into burning wrecks on the edge of the airfield.

The following day, sorties continued, but with the enemy rapidly approaching, orders were received for the ground personnel of 4 Squadron to leave Ronchin for Boulogne. The first echelon, under the command of Fg Off King, left Ronchin in nine lorries, which on arrival at Merville were unloaded and sent back to Ronchin for the second echelon. Just as the first echelon was about to leave Merville,

(4 Squadron records)

it came under attack from ten He 111s, and the airmen were lucky to escape unscathed on this occasion. Despite the roads being jammed with refugees, King made it to Boulogne in good time, only to receive further orders to move to Clairmarais (Klaarmares) near St Omer. At 0300hrs on 21 May, the first echelon arrived to prepare for further operations from Clairmarais.

The Germans had now advanced to within artillery range of Ronchin, and, by the end of 21 May, Ronchin had been relegated to an ALG. 4 Squadron still managed to fly several tactical reconnaissance sorties during the day. Once again, though, this came at a cost, and two more Lysanders were lost, the first, at 0800hrs, was from 'B' Flight at Ronchin. Plt Off P. M. Peace and Cpl R. A. Tamblin were shot down by a Bf 109 of 3./JG77, crashing at Bruyelle, near Tournai; Lt Hohoff claimed the kill. The other loss of the day occurred after Plt Off T. J. F. Davey and LAC J. H. Gillham were taking off from Clairmarais. Their Lysander Mk II, N1296, was brought down by a trio of Do 215s, which were about to attack St Omer. These would thankfully be the last aircrew fatalities, but unfortunately worse was to come for those on the ground.

Dunkirk beckons

It was now time to get away from Ronchin, and, at 0100hrs on 22 May, a convoy of ground personnel were ordered to make for Dunkirk. En-route, they were attacked at least six times by He 111s, and as the convoy got closer to Dunkirk, a large formation of Ju 87s seemed to single out the 4 Squadron contingent. They carried out a deadly, accurate attack, killing many of the 4 Squadron personnel and destroying a large amount of equipment. Those who survived, now under the command of WO Wallace, buried their colleagues in a field beside the still-burning remains of their transport and continued on foot. By 0830hrs, they finally arrived in Dunkirk to find a port that had been pounded by the Luftwaffe, and the sky was almost black with the smoke from burning oil tanks. That evening, the survivors were taken aboard the SS *St Helier* and moved to the safety of Dover later that evening.

The surviving aircraft of 'B' and 'C' Flights, now under the command of Flt Lt Campbell-Voullaire, left Ronchin and headed for Clairmarais, where they hoped they could continue the fight. The Lysanders took off at 0600hrs during a lull in the shelling, only to run into a formation of over 50 enemy aircraft, made up of Do17s, escorted by Bf 109s and Bf110s. Scattering in all directions, the Lysanders were lucky to escape, but this marked the end of the two flights' effectiveness in this campaign. The day ended with the 'A' Flight groundcrew and HQ section making it to Clairmarais, with just three serviceable aircraft remaining together with the remnants of 'A' Flight, 13 Squadron, which was now working with 4 Squadron, having suffered similar losses.

(4 Squadron records)

Remarkable escape

One of the aircraft that escaped the melee near Ronchin was the Lysander of Plt Off G. Scott and LAC 'Paddy' McAleese. They ended up making an unscheduled stop at an airfield near St Pol to be greeted by an army major who told them that the airfield had been evacuated. The major seized the opportunity to make use of the Lysander for some German tank spotting, as they had been reported in the area. Without hesitation, Scott took off again to look for the enemy but failed to find them so returned to St Pol. As they approached the airfield, the Germans found them, and the Lysander was riddled with machine gun fire. With the throttle wide open and now with a rough sounding engine, Scott managed to escape the enemy fire but, once clear, made a forced landing to have a closer look at the damage. At least 23 bullet holes were counted throughout the aircraft, including a hole in one of the Bristol Perseus' nine cylinders. Both airmen repaired the Lysander as well as they could, but with the light fading, the duo decided to stay the night with their battle-damaged aircraft. The following morning, they were hastily wakened by a Frenchman who told them that German tanks were less than a mile away and closing in fast. Both airmen leapt aboard the Lysander and quickly prepared to take off, but, much to the frustration of Scott, the aircraft's battery had drained overnight and the engine would not turn. Scott kept trying frantically to start the engine while McAleese prepared for imminent death or at best captivity. Miraculously, with the German tanks just a few hundred yards away the Perseus burst into life, and, literally under the enemy's gaze, the Lysander clambered into the air. A few more holes were added, but Scott and McAleese escaped again with very few options left other than to make for England. They found sanctuary at Ford in Sussex, and, with only a small amount of fuel remaining, Scott taxied up to the airfield's watch office. The shabby, tired looking Lysander was refuelled, and, after a few phone calls, Scott discovered that other 4 Squadron machines were congregating at Hawkinge. By now, Scott and McAleese were as tired as their aircraft, but this did not stop an officious, white-coated civilian demanding the crew pay 7s 6d in landing fees! Their reply was not recorded, but I'm sure it wasn't a polite one! On arrival at Hawkinge, they found the airfield in chaos, and the flying controller, despite what they had just been through, tried to persuade them to return across the Channel with a load of supplies for troops in Calais. Thankfully, official orders were received for the remains of 4 Squadron to reorganise at Detling, and by the 24 May 1940 the squadron, or what was left of it, was safely away from the fighting, at Ringway.

'B' Flight was still in France on 24 May, with the intention of continuing reconnaissance sorties from Clairmarais. However, the situation was rapidly deteriorating, and the airfield was about to be overrun by enemy tanks. By 0430hrs, the airfield was evacuated with both the aircraft and groundcrew heading for Dunkirk while Wg Cdr Charles and Plt Off Falconer remained behind to destroy anything of potential use to the enemy, including 5,000 gallons of aviation fuel and the squadron's trusty DH.89. On arrival at Dunkirk, the 4 Squadron Lysanders crossed the Channel for Hawkinge. The groundcrew eventually managed to escape onboard HMS *Wild Swan*, and a few days later all were reunited at Ringway.

During those few days in May 1940, 4 Squadron had managed to fly 106 operational sorties with the loss of 18 aircrew and 12 Lysanders destroyed. It was the groundcrew who suffered most of all though, being under fire throughout the majority of the month and suffering terrible losses during the attempt to reach Dunkirk; casualties were recorded at approximately 60 per cent! At least one other groundcrew died of his injuries in England, and three more were recorded as missing before the evacuation of Dunkirk was completed on 25 June 1940. The squadron had definitely earned its battle honour while supporting the BEF during those desperate few days trying to slow the advance of the German military machine.

4 Squadron lost 14 Lysanders during the Battle of France between early March and late June 1940. Eleven of these were lost between 13 May and 21 May 1940! (Via Martyn Chorlton)

4 SQUADRON LYSANDER LOSSES DURING THE BATTLE OF FRANCE

9 March 1940	L6852	Crash landing at Lille-Rochin; Plt Off W. B. Adamson + and LAC Satchell (OK)
16 April 1940	L4750	Crashed in take-off at Padville; Plt Off A. F. B. Ramsey + and LAC J. H. Gillham (OK)
13 May 1940	P9063	Shot down; Plt Off P. W. Vaughan and AC 2 E. Mold +
14 May 1940	P1711	Crashed nr Aspelaere ALG; Plt Off Hankey and Sgt Lewis (OK)
14 May 1940	L4742	Shot down; Fg Off T. C. Clarke and AC 1 W. S. Rodulson +
14 May 1940	L4745	Missing; Plt Off D. M. Barbour and Cpl R. H. Waters +
16 May 1940	L4814	Force landed nr Louvain; Plt Off Langley and LAC J. H. Gillham (OK)
16 May 1940	P9064	FTR/Missing; Fg Off E. E. Wood + and Cpl J. Bower (OK)
18 May 1940	N1263	Shot down; Fg Off E. C. Ford and Fg Off K. W. Graham +
19 May 1940	?	Shot down; Plt Off J. A. Plumb and LAC R. J. Thornton +
19 May 1940	N1305	Shot down; Fg Off L. J. Oldacres and LAC C. Butterill +
21 May 1940	N1296	Shot down; Plt Off T. J. F. Davey and LAC J. H. Gillham +
21 May 1940	N1298	Shot down; Plt Off P. M. Peace and Cpl R. A. Tamblin +
28 June 1940	P1733	Crashed nr Wiggington; Plt Off A. B. Corbett and AG (OK)

A groundcrew member fits an F.24 camera into a 4 Squadron Lysander only weeks before the beginning of the Battle of France. The peaceful 'Phoney War' period was brought to an abrupt end from mid-May 1940. (Topical Press Agency)

Reformed at Old Sarum on 1 April 1924, 16 Squadron remained a dedicated army co-operation unit for almost two decades initially with the F.2b, Atlas and Audax before receiving the Lysander Mk I in May 1938. This peaceful scene, most likely before the outbreak of the war, shows a Leading Aircraftman taking down a message using a portable radio transmitter. (*Aeroplane*)

Chapter 3

The 'Lizzie's' Bare Bones

The unconventional, built conventionally

On paper, the description of this two-seat single-engine high-wing monoplane sounds quite unremarkable. Its construction incorporated traditional, established Westland methods of aircraft manufacturing. However, the Lysander was a unique and complex looking machine, and its appearance was of a purely practical aircraft that accomplished exactly what it was originally

Above: The second prototype Westland P.8, K6128, in skeletal form at Yeovil in mid-1936. (Owen Cooper)

Below left: The cockpit of the Westland Lysander was dominated by the pilot's six vital instruments contained within the central panel. From top left to bottom right they are: the ASI (air speed indicator); artificial horizon; rate-of-climb indicator, altimeter, direction indicator and the turn-and-bank indicator. (Owen Cooper)

Below right: The right-hand side of the Lysander's instrument panel contains engine pressure and boost gauges such as the fuel pressure gauge, boost gauge, RPM indicator, oil pressure gauge and oil temperature gauge. The switchbox, visible on the extreme right, contains the switches for the navigation lamps, gun heating and pitot-head heating. (Owen Cooper)

designed to do – army co-operation missions with the ability to take off and land in a very small area. Its robustness would later lend itself to attacking land or maritime targets, Air-Sea Rescue (ASR) and the rigours of target towing.

Fuselage

The fuselage was built in two sections, fore and aft, which were joined together by bolted flat plates. The forward section, from the engine bulkhead to the rear cockpit, was made of square-sectioned duralumin tubes, joined together by gusset bolted plates or U-section extrusions. The rear section was constructed with welded steel tubes and the entire fuselage was assembled using Westland's established and conventional boxed girder construction.

The fuselage shape of the Lysander was achieved using wooden formers and stringers, which were all fabric covered. Along the starboard side of fuselage, running from the engine bulkhead to the rear cockpit, were generously sized panels that allowed access for general maintenance and inspection; this was always appreciated by the groundcrews, especially in the field.

The crew were accommodated under a lengthy greenhouse-type canopy, which gave both airmen an excellent field of vision in all directions. The pilot's position forward of the wing was fitted with a rearward sliding roof and sliding side windows, and was accessed via steps on the port undercarriage leg and enclosed in the fuselage. The canopy extended through to the observer's position, which was also fitted with a sliding window in the roof and was accessed using a pair of enclosed steps on the starboard side. The rear cockpit was fitted with hinged floor panels, which gave access to a bomb sight, bomb switches, a tail drift sight and the message hook.

The pilot and observer were separated by a superstructure shaped like a pylon to which the wing spars were connected. The pilot was protected by an armour-plated bulkhead behind his seat and a second armour plate behind the rear cockpit.

The left-hand side of the pilot's cockpit is dominated by the throttle box; the main throttle lever is at the top, and below is the engine mixture lever. Behind is the flap locking lever (appears to be disconnected in this shot) and below is the important large tailplane incidence hand wheel. (Owen Cooper)

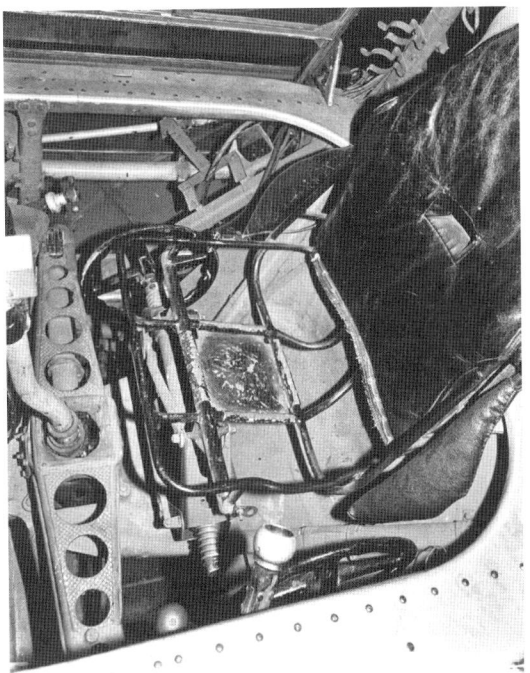

Above left: The pilot's seat, with padding removed, reveals the seat-adjusting hand wheel on the far side. (Owen Cooper)

Above right: The control column, complete with gun firing button (one of many different types fitted to the 'Lizzie'), and just obscured by the grip is the aircraft's brake operated lever. (Owen Cooper)

A standard Air Ministry Type P10 compass is fitted into this Lysander. This was the most common type of compass used by the RAF during World War Two and beyond, and it could be found in most types from the Tiger Moth to the Lancaster. (Owen Cooper)

The starboard instrument panel in the rear cockpit of a Lysander included the battery ammeter, charge regulating switch, voltmeter, and battery ammeter gauges along the bottom of the panel. (Owen Cooper)

Wings

The Lysander's unique wing design gave the aircraft unrivalled low-speed performance and handling. It was fitted to the fuselage via pin-joints attached to a Cabane strut within the fuselage structure. Inboard, the wing had a reversed, tapered leading edge and a straight trailing edge. The outboard section was the opposite. The 'D' sectioned main spar was made from Hiduminium with extruded sections machined into flanges, all joined by a flat plate stiffened with riveted sections. Attached to the riveted sections were the leading ribs, which were then covered in sheet metal to create a 'D' section leading edge torsion box. The main ribs were made of light alloy and were fabric-covered. At the rear of the main spar was a triangulated drag bracing made up of square section light alloy and tubes made of steel. These tubes were attached to a light or 'false' rear spar, to which the flaps and ailerons were attached. Only the leading edge to the main spar was covered in metal, all other wing surfaces were covered in fabric.

Both wings were supported by a pair of substantial 'Y-shaped' bracing struts, which attached to the underside at the point where the chord was at its deepest. The bottom end of each strut is shackled to the main undercarriage legs.

Along the full length of each leading edge were three-section slats, which operated along rollers on three runners in the main spar. Each was mounted on adjustable fittings, so that the correct setting of space between the slat and the wing could be set. The slats had pneumatic dampers as well to remove oscillations. The two outer flap sections operated independently of the inner ones. Handley Page flaps, positioned on the inner trailing edge, were connected to the inboard slats and raised up and down automatically. The ailerons were statically and dynamically balanced, of all-metal construction and fabric-covered.

Undercarriage

The cantilever undercarriage was constructed from a single length of hollow aluminium, which was bent into a horseshoe shape. The Dowty internally sprung wheels, fitted with Dunlop tyres, were mounted on stub axles and were joined to the forward fuselage by A-shaped fittings and bolts. The wheels were faired over with large, streamlined spats, which had a removable panel to expose the entire wheel and tyre to allow for changing and access to the Dunlop braking system. The faired legs concealed cables, fluid lines and the ammunition chutes, and, on the port side, footsteps enabled the pilot to access the cockpit. Harley landing lights, one on each side, were fitted into the front of the wheel spats.

The tail wheel was a Dunlop Ecta with a Dowty shock absorber, which could castor and self-centre. The Mk IIIA differed by having a Lockheed tail wheel unit with a slightly bigger tyre.

A Lysander pilot checks that his Mk VB Parachute Supply Container is firmly attached to a Mk 1 Light Series Carrier under the port stub wing. (Owen Cooper)

Left: The port side of the rear cockpit with the rear of the auxiliary fuel tank, located between the two crew, visible on the extreme left. At the top, the port rear cabane structure to which the rear spar is connected can be seen. (Owen Cooper)

Below: Another view of the rear cockpit and the rear of the auxiliary fuel tank, which was directly above the main 95-gallon De Bergue Semape self-sealing aluminium fuel tank. The auxiliary fuel tank could raise the endurance of the Lysander to eight hours. (Owen Cooper)

Powerplant

Power for the Mk I and Mk III was provided by the Bristol Mercury nine-cylinder, air-cooled, single-row piston radial engine. Designed by Roy Fedden of the Bristol Aeroplane Company, this highly successful powerplant went on to be fitted in 42 different aircraft. The unit used in the Mk I was the 890hp Mercury XII supercharged engine, which drove an 11ft, two-pitch de Havilland three-bladed propeller.

The Lysander Mk II was powered by the equally successful Bristol Perseus engine, also designed by Fedden. The Perseus differed from the Mercury XII by taking advantage of the sleeve valve principle enabling the engine to operate at higher speeds, in theory allowing a smaller sized unit to produce the same power as a larger one and with more efficiency. The Perseus saw RAF service with the Botha, Flamingo and Vildebeest, FAA service in the Roc and Skua, and civilian service in the Empire boats and Scylla. The Mk II used the 905hp Perseus XII, driving the same propeller as the Mk I.

The final main Lysander variant, the Mk III, used the 870hp Mercury XX or 30 engines, once again driving the same de Havilland propeller as the other marks. The Mercury 30, the penultimate in this range of engines, only differed by having a few crankshaft modifications. Later developed into another Bristol engine success story – the Pegasus – approximately 20,700 Mercury engines were built, and production did not end until 1945.

The cockpit of the Imperial War Museum's Lysander IIIA, V9673, before it was strung from the roof of Airspace Exhibition Hall, pictured in February 2004. (Via Martyn Chorlton)

A Lysander of 16 Squadron receives a minor service between sorties during an exercise from Old Sarum in 1939. 16 Squadron was first formed at Old Sarum when the Co-operation Squadron of the School of Army Co-operation was redesignated on 1 April 1924. Initially equipped with the F.2B Fighter, the Atlas followed in 1931, the Audax in 1933 and the Lysander from May 1938. (*Aeroplane*)

LYSANDER MK I, II AND III

Type
Single-engine, two-seat, high-wing army co-operation and/or ground support monoplane.

Powerplant
(Mk I) one 890hp Bristol Mercury XII 9-cylinder, air-cooled, supercharged radial engine; (Mk II) one 905hp Bristol Perseus XII; (Mk III) one 870hp Bristol Mercury XX or 30.

Dimensions
Span: 50ft
Length: 30ft 6in
Height: 14ft 6in
Gross wing area: 260sq ft

Weights
Empty: (Mk I) 4,044lb; (Mk II) 4,160lb; (Mk III) 4,365lb
Max take-off: (Mk I) 5,920lb; (Mk II) 6,030lb; (Mk III) 6,330lb; (Mk IIIA[SD]) 10,000lb

Performance
Max speed at sea level: (Mk I) 211mph; (Mk II) 206mph; (Mk III) 209mph
Max speed at 10,000ft: (Mk I) 219mph; (Mk II) 230mph; (Mk III) 207mph
Minimum flying speed: (Mk I and II) 54mph; (Mk III) 56mph
Max dive speed: (All marks) 300mph
Rate of climb to 10,000ft: (Mk I and II) 6.9 mins; (Mk III) 8 mins
Service ceiling: (Mk I and II) 26,000ft; (Mk III) 21,500ft
Take-off run to 50ft: (Mk I) 250 yards; (Mk II) 245 yards; (Mk III) 305 yards
Landing run from 50ft: (Mk I) 310 yards; (Mk II) 330 yards; (Mk III) 340 yards
Range on internal fuel: 600 miles at 150mph; (III[SD]) 450-mile radius of action

Armament
Gun armament: A pair of free-firing .303in Browning machine guns in wheel-spats and a single or a pair of Lewis machine guns in the rear cockpit. Option for a pair of 20mm Oerlikon or Hispano cannon in lieu of stub winglets.

Bomb armament: Up to two 250lb GP/HE, four 112lb Mk VII GP/HE or eight 20lb HE bombs carried on stub winglets (Universal No.1 Carrier); four 20lb bombs carried under fuselage on a Light Series Mk I Bomb Carrier 'Toast Rack'. Option of a SBC (Small Bomb Container) designed to carry 4lb, 25lb and 30lb IBs.

External Stores
Two M-Type dinghy containers and four smoke markers; two SCI (Smoke Curtain Installation) canisters; two Mk VB parachute supply droppers; a single 150-gallon long-range fuel for the Mk IIIA(SD).

Some of the paraphernalia that accompanied an army co-operation squadron, in front of one of Old Sarum's World War One hangars in the summer of 1940. There is every chance that this RAF wireless van, belonging to 16 Squadron, was abandoned in France during its rapid withdrawal in May 1940. (*Aeroplane*)

A line of 2 Squadron Lysander Mk Is at Hawkinge in late 1938, loaded with Mk VB parachute supply droppers under their stub wings. The RAF's pioneering Army Co-operation Squadron first received the Lysander in July 1938 and retained the type until July 1942 although long before, the Tomahawk and Mustang were already on strength. (*Aeroplane*)

Chapter 4

The Lysander at War

The phoniest of wars

It was in the middle of a large mobilisation exercise that 50 (Army Co-operation) Wing at Odiham was ordered to prepare for war for real on 23 August 1939. From that day onwards, the personnel of all Lysander squadrons knew that they were the most likely to be sent across the Channel in support of the army. On the declaration of war at 1100hrs on 3 September, all Lysander units were on tenterhooks, but they would clearly not be advanced into France until the BEF, which they would

Taken at the height of the 'Phoney War' in December 1939, this image belied what lay ahead for the Lysander units in France and to a lesser, but equally costly extent, for the Hurricane squadrons too. (Barrat's Photo Press via *Aeroplane*)

support, was in position. Two weeks later, the ground parties of 4 and 13 Squadrons were ordered to move by train to Portsmouth and onwards by sea to Cherbourg. It was then a long train journey to Monchy-Lagache.

The aircraft of 4 and 13 Squadrons both left Odiham on 24 September, landing at Mons-en-Chaussée the same day. While 13 Squadron remained at Mons-en-Chaussée, 4 Squadron moved to Monchy-Lagache. The second pair of Lysander units, which were part of 51 (Army Co-operation) Wing, 2 Squadron and 26 Squadron, arrived at Abbeville/Drucat on 29 September and 3 October, respectively. The Lysanders that would support the BEF during their campaign in France had now been fully deployed.

While the German forces recovered following their success in the east, very little activity occurred during the first few months of the war, hence the popular title for this period being 'The Phoney War'. Faith in holding back the enemy was over-confidently placed in the Maginot Line, although the BEF had no such luxury, as they were deployed along the exposed French/Belgian border. The scene was now set, with the two Lysander wings attempting to cover the same area that needed over 20 RFC and Royal Naval Air Service (RNAS) squadrons to cover it just over 20 years earlier.

Back in Britain, additional Lysander units were in the making when 614 Squadron moved to Odiham on 2 October. The auxiliary squadron's 'B' Flight was used to briefly create 614A Squadron on 9 October, which, in turn, provided the nucleus for the latest Lysander unit, 225 Squadron. 613 (City of Manchester) Squadron also moved into Odiham on 2 October with the Hector and Hind, but it was not destined to receive the Lysander until April 1940.

16 Squadron was prepared for service in France after it had moved closer to a war footing by moving from Old Sarum to Hawkinge on 17 February. On 13 April, the squadron crossed the Channel bound for Amiens and settling at Bertangles the following day. During April, squadron strength remained at 12 Lysanders, but this was increased to 18, giving each unit the ability to operate a three-flight system, rather than the traditional two. Squadron aircraft serviceability was a credit to the groundcrews during this period as well, despite being handicapped by the fact that all maintenance was performed outdoors, regardless of the weather.

4 Squadron during peacetime manoeuvres from Odiham in 1939. Only a few months after this photo was taken, the unit joined 13 Squadron to become the first Lysander units in France. (Via *Aeroplane*)

A Lysander Mk II of 13 Squadron has its Perseus XII sleeve-valve engine warmed through at Mons-en-Chassée during the winter of 1939/1941, when the 'Phoney War' was at its height. (Via Martyn Chorlton)

Battle of France

In late April, the 51st (Highland) Division was repositioned on the Maginot Line, and the French requested that the RAF supply close air support of the region. A combined unit of 2 Squadron's Lysanders and 87 Squadron's Hurricanes were moved to Spincourt on 5 May but had barely settled in when the German forces began their attack on 10 May. With haste, the short-lived combined unit was withdrawn back to its original airfields in preparation.

At this stage, deployment was as follows; 50 Wing at Athies, under the command of Gp Capt A. R. Churchman, DFC, controlled 4, 13 and 16 squadrons, while 51 Wing at Dieppe, commanded by Wg Cdr A. H. Flower, CBE, was in charge of 2 and 26 squadrons.

A large German attack via Belgium was already being prepared for, and a prearranged plan to move the BEF forward to a position in line with the River Dyle was instigated. This left the nearest Lysander units over 50 miles away from the frontline, and even though all of the squadrons were preparing ALGs, very few were ready.

26 Squadron was the first to be involved in the German Blitzkrieg, when the Luftwaffe bombed Dieppe, forcing the unit's Lysanders into the air, rather than risk their destruction on the ground. Other units began the task of flying over the new BEF lines and photographing them, which inevitably involved encounters with enemy aircraft. 4 Squadron had their first contact with the enemy on 13 May by Plt Off B. Malins and LAC 'Ginger' Drew, who made it back to Ronchin after receiving some unwanted attention from several German anti-aircraft guns. As the Lysanders encountered an ever-increasing number of enemy fighters, it was only a matter of time before the first casualty was recorded. Fg Off P. W. Vaughan and his air gunner AC E. Mold in P9063 became the first casualties recorded after they failed to return from a tactical reconnaissance after leaving Monchy-Lagache at 0730hrs.

On 15 May, it was decided that 4 Squadron should move forward to Ronchin while still maintaining detachments at Aspelaere and Clairmarais. By midday on 16 May, the move was complete, with

'B' Flight now operating from the ALG at Aspelaere. 'B' Flight found itself covering the massed withdrawal of 2 Corp, and it was another frantic day of action for 4 Squadron. Plt Off Langley and his air gunner, LAC J. H. Gillham, came under attack from six Bf110s while flying an observation sortie near Louvain. Despite the odds, Gillham claimed to have shot down one of the fighters before their aircraft, L4814, force-landed near Lille.

By 19 May, the German advance was at the point of overrunning the BEF's Air Component airfields. The inevitable withdrawal of the Lysander squadrons was now being controlled from across the Channel, as communications with HQ, British Air Forces in France had completely broken down. 2, 13, 16 and 26 squadrons were ordered to withdraw to airfields in the southeast of England, which were given the codename 'Back Violet', while those that remained in France were ordered to move to the lower Seine area, codenamed 'South Violet'. 2 Squadron was the first to withdraw via Boulogne on 19 May, arriving at Lympne the following day and then settling at Bekesbourne for duties still in support of the BEF. The rapidly depleting 4 Squadron was withdrawn from its ALGs to Clairmarais on 21 May, losing two more aircraft to Bf 109s in the process. By the following day, the remnants of the squadron were at Dunkirk and 4 Squadron was now effectively out of the battle.

Some army co-operation support was still available to the BEF across the Channel, as 13 Squadron joined 2 Squadron on 29 May, and 16 and 26 Squadrons were operational at Lympne. Following the complete withdrawal of 4 Squadron, which by 24 May was at Ringway, it was replaced by 613 Squadron, which was detached from Odiham to Hawkinge. Along with the other Lysander units, 613 Squadron took part in supply drops of food, water and ammunition to BEF troops at Calais.

From right to left; Fg Off Scotter, LAC Evans and LAC Gill attempt to start the Mercury XII nine-cylinder engine of a 2 Squadron Lysander Mk I at Abbeville in October 1939. Having suffered heavy losses, the squadron left France on 16 May 1940. (Via Martyn Chorlton)

Armed tactical reconnaissance sorties were also flown by 16, 26 and 613 squadrons while the BEF began its evacuation from the beaches at Dunkirk. Those forces that did not make for Dunkirk headed for Cherbourg instead, but even at this late stage not all of the RAF had evacuated the area. Sqn Ldr T. K. Lacey was in charge of a small section at Rouen Boos airfield, and from 23 May into early June, he directed regular reconnaissance operations with a few Blenheims and Lysanders. By 3 June, this enclave of the RAF was taken over by 10 Air Intelligence Liaison Section, which ordered the remaining aircraft to carry out a tactical reconnaissance of Somme bridges and enemy positions near Abbeville. Two Lysanders were involved in what was to be their last operation over France; one failed to return, the last of 62 Lysanders lost in France out of the 90 originally on strength, while a further 17 were SOC. 13 and 26 squadrons alone had lost 23 pilots and air gunners and 35 aircraft between them in the space of four weeks!

Anti-invasion

After the dispersal of the Lysander squadrons operating from 'Back Violet' airfields, all thoughts were focused on how Britain could stop the Germans from invading. Lysanders now found themselves being used for armed coastal patrols along the south and east coasts of the country. Several flights were allocated phosphorous bombs, which, at various points along the coast, would be dropped into fuel that had been pumped into the sea; one of a multitude of anti-invasion ideas. Several Lysander stations were also stocked with gas bombs in case the Germans used chemical weapons during the invasion.

The Lysander was also heavily involved in the problem of Ireland, which was neutral during World War Two. Britain was fearful that the Germans would use the country as a stepping stone to attack Northern Ireland and then move on to the mainland. 416 Flight, based in Northern Ireland, was formed with Lysanders to support the many British soldiers based in the country, and Ireland also bought the type for its own coastal patrol duties.

By now, there was no shortage of Lysanders available in Britain, but the Ministry of Aircraft Production (MAP) decided by mid-1940 that all focus should be on fighter and bomber production and not army co-operation machines. Despite attempts to expand Lysander production to Doncaster, Yeovil production continued with the Mercury XX-powered Mk III.

Various ideas were proposed and trialled by Westland for specialist 'anti-invasion' Lysanders, but once the threat had passed, all thoughts turned back to the idea of taking the fight back to the enemy. With this in mind, three new Lysander units were formed in September 1940. First was 239 Squadron at Hatfield on 18 September from flights provided by 16 and 225 squadrons. Next was 241 Squadron on 25 September at Longman from the 'A' Flights of 4 and 614 squadrons, and finally 268 Squadron on 30 September at Bury St Edmunds from 2 and 26 squadrons. The one and only allied Lysander squadron formed a few days later at Abbotsinch on 7 October in the shape of 309 (Ziemia Czerwienska) Squadron, specifically to carry out army co-operation training for Polish forces based in Scotland.

This resurgence of Lysander units helped to bring about the formation of Army Co-operation Command on 17 November under the control of Air Marshal Sir A. S. Barrett, KCB, CMG, MC. Army Co-operation Command was divided into two groups: 70 (Training) Group, which looked after anti-aircraft co-operation units (AACU) and 41 and 42 (Army Co-operation) Operational Training Units (OTU) and several target-towing flights (TTF) based at Old Sarum and Andover; and 71 (Army Co-operation) Group, which controlled the activities of 2, 4, 13, 16, 26, 225, 231, 239, 241, 268, 309, 613 and 614 squadrons.

However, despite the large organisation, the Lysander had become the subject of serious questions regarding the aircraft's capability as an army co-operation machine. Following the Battle of Britain,

Polish groundcrew of 309 (Ziema Czerwienska) Squadron remove a Williamson F.24 camera from Lysander Mk IIIA V9437, at Dunino in 1941. Formed at Abbotsinch with the Lysander Mk III on 7 October 1940, the Polish unit operated the 'Lizzie' until the arrival of the Mustang Mk I in August 1942. (Via Martyn Chorlton)

senior staff had time to analyse the lessons of France, and it was clear that an aircraft with the performance and armament of a fighter was required for the role. What had been asked of the Lysander were two completely different tasks, namely artillery spotting and reconnaissance, which were totally incompatible. The result was that the Lysander found itself being replaced by four different types; the Tomahawk and Mustang took over the fighter reconnaissance, and the loitering air observation work was now carried out by the Auster and Taylorcraft.

The Western Desert

The first Lysanders to arrive in the Middle East were crated and despatched to Heliopolis in November 1938. The 24 aircraft, serialled L4707 to L4730, were re-assembled, and, the following month, two of them were collected by 6 Squadron, based at Ramleh, for evaluation in the anti-terrorist role. At the same time, 208 Squadron was preparing to convert from the Audax to the Lysander at Heliopolis, a task that was complete by January 1939.

Another two-dozen Lysanders arrived at Heliopolis in mid-1939 to cover those already in service with 208 Squadron and the pair that remained with 6 Squadron. By September 1939, 6 Squadron received a full quota of Lysanders to complement the Hardys and Gauntlet fighters it had acquired the previous month.

On the outbreak of war in Europe, both squadrons expected to be shipped back to Britain, but the commander-in-chief, RAF Middle East, was adamant that his army co-operation units should stay with the army units that they had exercised with. This was a wise move, because when Mussolini saw the success the Germans had achieved in France, he brought forward his plans to invade Egypt and declared war on Britain and France on 10 June 1940.

As part of 202 Group, the Lysanders of 208 Squadron were quickly in action tasked with monitoring the enemy's forward positions. Fighter protection was provided for them, but losses still occurred, such as on 22 June, when one of three escorting Gladiators was shot down by CR.42s. Lysanders still managed to score some successes against the enemy, a good example of which occurred on 11 July, when a single machine was looking for a missing patrol from the 11th Hussars. The Lysander crew saw an Italian aircraft landing in the desert to help another downed machine, east of El Adem. The 208 Squadron pilot dived down with his front guns blazing, and, as he pulled away, the air gunner opened up as well. The Lysander kept circling above as the Italian aircrew scattered across the desert. After more gun fire, both enemy aircraft caught fire, giving the Lysander crew a double victory.

On 10 November, a 208 Squadron Lysander was photographing Maktila camp when the air gunner spotted half a dozen CR.42s, climbing rapidly, 5,000ft below. The Lysander pilot made a rapid turn for home as the CR.42s began their attack in a line astern formation. The air gunner never gave up firing, despite being wounded in the leg, while the pilot headed for the deck so that the enemy fighters could not attack the Lysander's blind spot. However, at only 100ft above the ground, the Lysander's engine gave up the ghost, and a forced landing quickly followed. As the Lysander touched the desert, the air gunner's relentless fire paid off and a CR.42 crashed alongside. The air gunner, whose leg had been broken, managed to get his injured pilot out of the wreckage, and, not long after, both were treated for their injuries by a nearby patrol from the 11th Hussars.

Reinforcements for the army co-operation role began to arrive by late 1940. First, 'C' Flight of 208 Squadron had its Lysanders replaced by tactical reconnaissance Hurricanes, while 3 (Royal Australian Air Force, RAAF) Squadron, recently arrived in theatre, was re-equipped with Lysanders. 6 Squadron was ordered to get ready for a move to the Western Desert, a unit that by now had 13 Lysanders on strength with their 'C' Flight. The flight was moved to Qasaba, Egypt, in September for operational training before moving forward to join 208 Squadron. 'C' Flight first saw action from 1 October and by December had rotated with 'B' Flight.

Lysander strength in North Africa was depleted from February 1941, when 208 Squadron was withdrawn to support allied forces in Greece, which was invaded by Italian forces from Albania. This left just 'A' and 'B' Flights of 6 Squadron at Tobruk under the direct control of HQ, 202 Group. The squadron HQ was moved to Heliopolis and 'C' Flight was re-equipped with long-range Lysanders in support of the planned invasion of the Dodecanese Islands, which never came to fruition. By March 1941, 'A' Flight had been re-equipped with Hurricanes at Agedabia for army co-operation with the 2nd Armoured Division, and 'B' Flight, retaining Lysanders, took over 208 Squadron's tasking at Barce.

Following Generalfeldmarschall (Field Marshal) Rommel's arrival, the British forces were pushed back into Egypt, but a large garrison held out at Tobruk and amongst their forces were the Lysanders and Hurricanes of 6 Squadron and a few Hurricanes from 73 Squadron. By 8 April, both squadrons were operating from El Gubbi East, but in an effort to disperse, 6 Squadron moved to El Gubbi West the following day. It was the same day that 6 Squadron achieved its last Lysander air-to-air victory, as Plt Off J. E. McFall and his air gunner, Cpl Copley, shot down a Ju52/3m during a long-range tactical reconnaissance operation.

Re-formed as an army co-operation unit from 'B' Flight of 614 Squadron at Odiham on 9 October 1939, 225 Squadron operated the Lysander Mk II and later Mk III until June 1942. Pictured in mid-1940, whilst operating from Tilshead, Mk II N1256 was transferred to 4 Squadron, Indian Air Force, but was destroyed near Kohat on 20 March 1942, following engine failure. (Rolls Royce via Martyn Chorlton)

One of 208 Squadron's first Lysanders, which was delivered in January 1939, was Mk I L4734. After brief service with 13 Squadron, the aircraft was returned to 208, only to be destroyed in an air raid at Palmyra on 10 July 1941. (Via Martyn Chorlton)

6 Squadron continued to hold out against constant bombing and strafing attacks until 19 April, when just four serviceable Lysanders and a Magister left Tobruk at night, bound for Maaten Bagush. After a sterling defence by the Hurricanes of 73 Squadron, which were now up against the Bf 109Es of JG.27, only four serviceable aircraft remained by 25 April, and these were forced to withdraw as well.

This was the last time the Lysander would be in the thick of it in the front line. Its operational role in the desert was, from this point forward, taken over by the Hurricane.

East Africa

In September 1940, 237 Squadron moved to Gordon's Tree, Khartoum, to help support the attack by allied forces on Abyssinia and Eritrea. The following month, the unit's Audaxes and Hardys were replaced by the Lysander Mk I and Mk II, complemented by Gladiators in March 1941. As the main RAF and South African Air Force offensive began, 237 Squadron joined in on 30 March when three aircraft dive-bombed a military barracks and buildings at Asmara. The following day, three more Lysanders dive-bombed an enemy motorised column, 50 miles south of Massawa.

By mid-May the bulk of the Italian forces surrendered, and 237 Squadron was moved to the Western Desert where all of the unit's Lysanders were replaced by the Hurricane Mk I in September 1941.

As far as East Africa was concerned, only the Lysanders of the Royal Egyptian Air Force (REAF) were in evidence, conducting anti-submarine patrols over the Red Sea. The only RAF Lysander unit was 1414 Meteorological Flight, based at Khartoum, which had moved to Egypt by early 1942.

However, the Lysander found one last use in the region following the alarming rate that the Japanese were advancing across Asia. There was a fear that Vichy-controlled Madagascar could be used as a base for the Japanese to launch attacks on Africa. In February 1942, the island was occupied by the British, and a token force of aircraft, including the Lysanders of 1433 Flight, were established at Diego Suarez from May 1942. The Lysander remained evident on Madagascar until April 1943.

Greece

The Lysander's contribution during the Greek campaign of 1941 was as quick as the German advance. 208 Squadron, having been withdrawn from North Africa, moved into its new theatre at Kazaklar on 6 April, immediately organising detachments to Larissa and Pharsala.

Once 208 Squadron had settled in, the German advance was already unstoppable, and, by 19 April, the unit was withdrawn to Elevsis on the outskirts of Athens. By this stage, only four Lysanders remained serviceable, and these were withdrawn to Argos on the island of Crete on 22 April. The unit's Hurricanes remained slightly longer in a brave attempt to provide some air defence, but by 28 April the entire squadron was withdrawn to Egypt, then Palestine, where it was re-equipped with the Audax.

The Far East

It was as early as March 1938 that the first of many Lysanders had appeared in India, and by the following year that country's air force prepared itself for a rapid expansion, which would include the Westland-built machine.

However, it was not until 1941 that 48 Lysanders were allocated to the Indian Air Force (IAF), the first arriving at the joint RAF/IAF depot at Drigh Road, Karachi. 1 (Indian) Squadron was moved from its northwest frontier posting by August to re-equip with the Lysander at Drigh Road. By the following month, a single flight was on its way back to Peshawar, and, apart from one minor landing accident en-route (which was repaired by groundcrew being carried in the rear cockpit), all of the Lysanders safely reached their operational airfield.

By November, the IAF 1 Squadron's 12 aircraft, which up to this point still belonged to the RAF, were officially handed over to the governor of Bombay during a ceremony at Peshawar. This would be the first of ten Lysander squadrons for the IAF, all of which would prove invaluable in support of the Allied Forces along the Indian border with Burma.

As the Japanese rapidly advanced through Burma, 1 (Indian) Squadron was moved to Magwe, the home of 28 Squadron on 1 February with Lysander Mk IIs. That evening, the Japanese Air Force bombed the airfield, but both squadrons escaped with only minor damage. In response, 1 (Indian) Squadron's commanding officer, Sqn Ldr Majumdar, believing the enemy to have come from Mae-Haugsaum in Siam, set out on 3 February to bomb the airfield alone, escorted by a pair of 67 Squadron Buffaloes. Majumdar attacked at low-level, dropping a pair of 250lb bombs on the only hangar on the airfield. The following day, Majumdar led a larger unescorted attack on the airfield.

With the Japanese advance, the Lysander units found themselves spread over a vast area, ranging from supporting the Chinese 5th Army to Mingaladon and the defence of Rangoon. Rough airfields were taking their toll on the Lysander population more than the enemy ever could, and several were destroyed when bombs were shaken from their carriers during the take-off run. Despite the efforts of the Lysander crews, the Allies were pushed back into India.

Following this withdrawal, Indian squadrons began to receive the Hurricane, including 1 (Indian) Squadron, while others continued to reform with the Lysander, such as 4 (Indian) Squadron on 16 February 1942. By the end of the year, 4 (Indian) Squadron was conducting army co-operation missions with the 7th Indian Division, but the Lysander in squadron service was rapidly coming to a close.

28 Squadron began re-equipping with the Hurricane from December 1942 and 20 Squadron, whose aircraft had been involved in the siege of Imphal, was re-equipped in January 1943.

In a scene reminiscent of the Battle of France (but with the positions reversed), a 208 Squadron Lysander pays a visit to El Adem, framed by a wrecked Italian Air Force machine. (Via Martyn Chorlton)

The prototype of the 'Long-Range' variant of the Lysander was Mk III, T1771, here at Boscombe Down at the beginning of Aeroplane and Armament Experimental Establishment (A&AEE) trials in June 1941. The aircraft's career was to be short-lived because after being delivered to 138 Squadron, it was destroyed by fire after it crashed into some trees in fog near Upper Holme, Hungry Hill, Farnham, Surrey. The crew, Flt Lt A. J. de V. Laurent and LAC J. A. Harkness, were killed. (Via Martyn Chorlton)

Formed in Britain in February 1942 with the Lysander Mk IIIA, 1433 Flight played an important role in preventing Madagascar potentially falling into Japanese hands and providing a gateway to the east coast of Africa. The flight operated from Diego Suarez, Maratsipoy, Ivato and Tananarive before disbanding on 15 April 1943. (Via Martyn Chorlton)

Another Lysander unit that managed to shy away from the camera a great deal was 28 Squadron, serving in India. The squadron operated the Lysander Mk II from September 1941 to December 1942, including N1273, which was wrecked at Kohat after taking off with coarse pitch settings on 19 December 1941. (Via Martyn Chorlton)

Chapter 5

The Aerial Pimpernel

Only one aircraft

Following the fall of the Low Countries and France in June 1940, no time was wasted in forming the Special Operations Executive (SOE) in London. Its main task was to work closely with the newly formed French underground movement, and agents and supplies could easily be dropped in using unmodified operational bombers. Getting them out was a different story, and the only aircraft capable of this was the Lysander.

By August 1940, a pair of Lysanders were made available for special duties (SD) operations and two more were held in reserve by 419 Flight, based at North Weald. In September, the flight moved to Stapleford Tawney, and on to Stradishall in October, and, from March 1941, Newmarket Heath was also used. By 1 March, the unit was redesignated as 1419 Flight with Lysanders, Whitleys and a single Maryland on strength.

The very first special duty operation took place in September 1941, when one agent was flown into France and another was returned, instantly proving that the Lysander was the perfect machine for the job. Pilots selected for these operations were usually very experienced and would have served with at least one army co-operation unit, although the majority seemed to have passed through 2 Squadron at Sawbridgeworth at some stage.

Lysanders were a fairly common sight at Boscombe Down during the later 1930s and early 1940s, but this one was a little different. This is the prototype Lysander Mk III 'Long-Range', T1771, during trials with the A&AEE in June 1941 and later referred to as the 'Special Duties' (SD) variant. The aircraft's long-range came from the substantial 150-gallon fuel tank mounted below the fuselage, which was originally designed to be carried internally by a Handley Page Harrow! (Via Martyn Chorlton)

Converted for special duties

Following the first successful forays into France, the Lysander became specially modified for the task, and 20 Mk IIIs and Mk IIIAs were taken from maintenance units for conversion. Under a special MAP contract, named Lysander SCW (Special Contract Westland), the modification work included fitting a 150-gallon long-range fuel tank and lightening the aircraft by removing all armament, armour and any fitting surplus to requirements in the rear cockpit. This made enough room for two agents in moderate comfort, three at a squeeze, and, if push came to shove, a fourth could lie on the floor. Their night role saw the special Lysanders' under-surfaces painted in a sooty non-reflective black paint, and a ladder was fitted on the port side of the fuselage below the rear cockpit, its steps painted in luminous paint. These modifications resulted in the aircraft being redesignated as the Mk III(SD), and the few that had armament and armour left in place were referred to as the Mk IIIA(SD).

A&AEE trials at Boscombe Down in June 1941 gave the SD a radius of action of 450 miles and a cruising speed of 165mph. More importantly, short field trials with four passengers saw the SD variant lift off the ground within 600 yards, while a normal load took less than half that distance.

Images of operational SD Lysanders are very rare, and even this photo of Mk IIIA (SD) V9287 was taken at Yeovil before delivery. This Lysander never served with an operational squadron. (Via Martyn Chorlton)

Behind enemy lines

While the tools of the trade were being prepared, 1419 Flight had outgrown itself and, on 25 August 1941, was redesignated 138 (Special Duties) Squadron at Newmarket under the command of Sqn Ldr J. Nesbitt-Dufort. Two days later, the Lysander Flight of 138 Squadron received its first operational pick-up order. The operation was to be carried out on the night of 4 September via Tangmere, where all SOE operations would be staged through during the war. Nesbitt-Dufort, in Lysander Mk III T1770, was ordered to deliver an agent by the name of Gerry Morel and collect another called J. T. P. M. Vaillant de Guelis. At 2300hrs, the Lysander took off from Tangmere and, at 14,000ft, crossed the enemy coast bound for Tours. Arriving over the prescribed destination at 0130hrs, Nesbitt-Dufort circled for 15 minutes, but no signal from the ground could be seen. It transpired that Guelis had been delayed after his papers had been checked and was frantically pedalling towards the collection point. Realising he was not going to make in time, Guelis decided to lay his marker torches in the field he was passing, knowing that Nesbitt-Dufort would be getting low on fuel. The Lysander pilot spotted the upturned torches, laid out in an 'L' shape, and in no time had put the aircraft down, then taxied back along the length of the 'L' in readiness for taking off again. In less than four minutes, Morel was on his way and Guelis prepared to leave France as Nesbitt-Dufort opened the throttle with full boost. The pilot aimed for a gap in the tree-shrouded field, which appeared to be just a hedge, but, as the Lysander flew over it, there was a blinding flash from a high-tension cable that was ripped down. The sturdy machine kept on flying back to Tangmere with no further problems.

Into enemy hands

Another hair-raising sortie, again involving Nesbitt-Dufort, took place on 28/29 January 1942 while flying Lysander Mk III T1508. Tasked with a two-passenger pick-up near Tours, all went well with the landing and take-off, but on return, near Bernay, at 7,000ft, a foreboding cold front made up of cumulonimbus clouds blocked the route home. With no chance of climbing over the cloud, Nesbitt-Dufort was forced to fly parallel with the front from east to west until an opportunity to push through presented itself. This never came, and with fuel rapidly disappearing, Nesbitt-Dufort decided to push through the black clouds. The inevitable turbulence began to throw the Lysander around, and ice rapidly formed on the wings. In no time at all, the aircraft became uncontrollable and began to lose height. Nesbitt-Dufort called on the intercom ordering his two passengers to bale out – but it later transpired that they were not plugged in! Diving rapidly restored control again, but by now the fuel was critical, and there was no chance of the Lysander making it across the Channel. Still covered in ice, Nesbitt-Dufort quickly found a suitable field to land in, but a high-speed approach saw the aircraft safely down only to overrun into a ditch and end up on its nose. The agents in the back of the aircraft jumped in exuberant mood thinking they had arrived in England! In the meantime, Nesbitt-Dufort was desperately trying to burn T1508, but there was so little fuel remaining in the tanks, this proved impossible. Forced to leave the Lysander intact, the trio made contact with the local underground, and they were soon hidden away from the enemy. However, the Germans now had in their possession an intact SD Lysander; while frustrating, this did not result in SD Lysander operations ending or changing in any way.

The momentum began to increase during 1942 with ten successful Lysander operations being conducted, entailing the delivery of 15 agents into, and 18 men and one woman out of, France. The year also saw 138 Squadron's Lysanders transfer to form 161 Squadron at Tempsford on 15 February. The unit flew a host of other types, but the Lysander would be the only one that would serve with the squadron until its disbandment in June 1945.

Originally built as a Mk IIIA and then converted to a TT Mk IIIA, V9289 later joined 'C' Flight of 357 Squadron as a Mk IIIA (SD). The aircraft was lost on 3 September 1945 when it crashed on Amherst Beach during a pick-up. (Via Martyn Chorlton)

Unmodified aircraft were also involved in special duties, including Mk I L4738. The aircraft served with the SD Flight, Boscombe Down, from 1940 until it was SOC on 21 June 1944. (Via Martyn Chorlton)

The Lysander's workload reached its peak in 1943, when 60 agents were delivered to France and 81 were brought back during 38 operations. The Special Duty Flight of 161 Squadron increased in size to nine aircraft, with another in reserve, during the year.

The first of 11 female agents, Francine Agazarian, was delivered by Lysander into France on 17 March 1943. Agazarian operated under the code-name 'Madeline' and unlike several of the others she returned back to England by Lysander in June 1943. Seven of the female agents were executed or died in captivity, while only two others survived, and only one other woman agent returned to England in a Lysander. Three further women agents who were parachuted into France were all returned to England by Lysander.

Following the Normandy invasion in June 1944, the need to drop agents into France began to reduce, and by September the majority of the country had been liberated. By this time, it was calculated that SD Lysanders had flown 43 operations at night over France, in 73 sorties. This would have meant that up to three Lysanders could have been operating over France on a single night. The final agent tally was 102 delivered to France and 129 brought out.

Special duties in the Mediterranean and the Far East

In February 1944, another clandestine squadron, 148, based at Brindisi, took the first of several Lysanders on strength for the SD role. The aircraft would prove very useful for tasking that involved landing behind enemy lines in Italy and liaising with partisans in Yugoslavia. Five more SD Lysanders were taken on before the year was over to help keep an eye on the unstable political situation in Greece.

Lysander Mk IIIA TT, V9815, of 357 Squadron, which was DBR in a heavy landing in Burma on 4 August 1945, only ten days before the Japanese finally surrendered.

Only identifiable as 'Z', this Lysander is about to embark on a sortie carrying eight 20lb Mk I bombs under each of its stub wings. The stub wing was the most versatile of attachments and a variety of stores could be carried below it. Other offensive configurations included four 112lb Mk VII bombs, four 120lb Mk I bombs or even a pair of 250lb bombs. (*Aeroplane*)

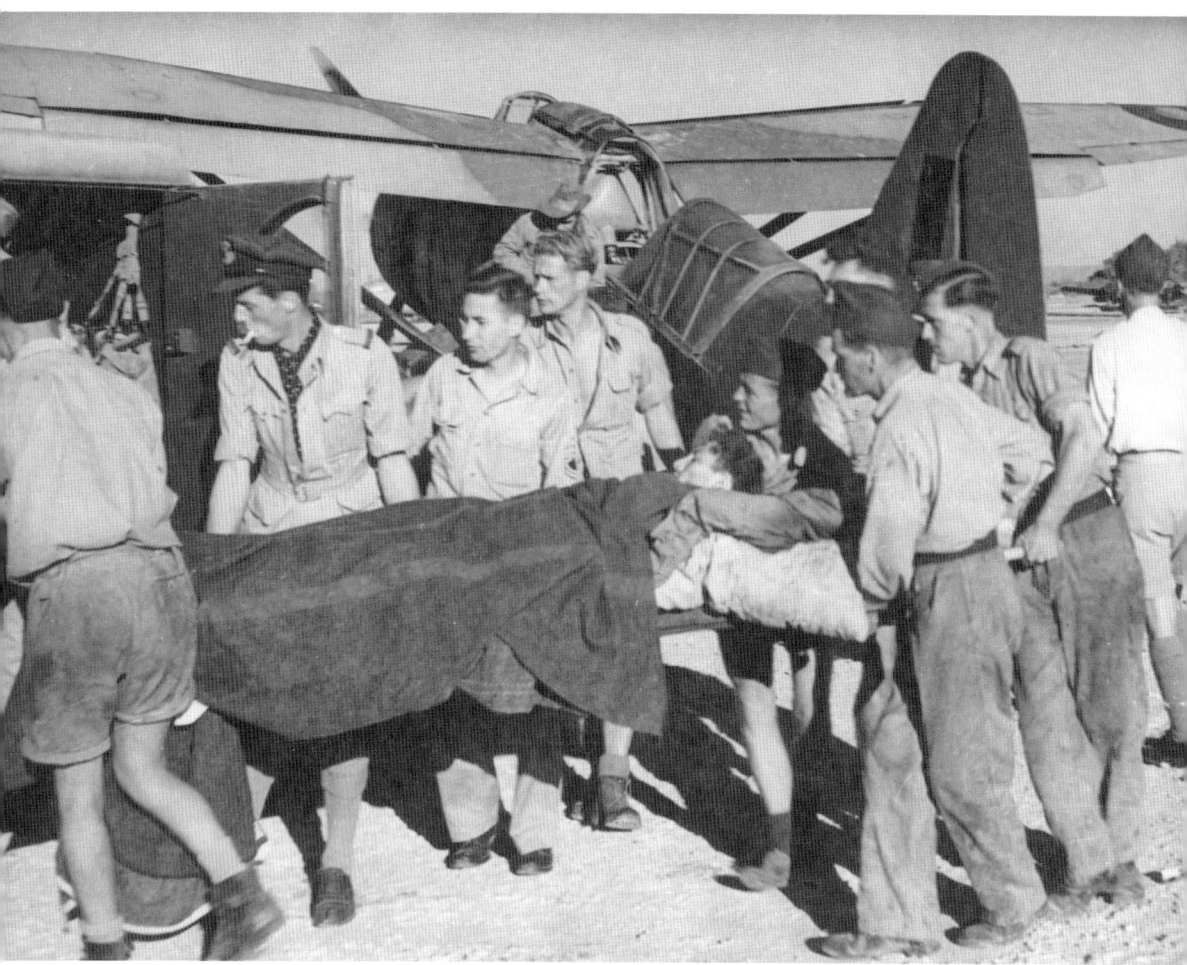

'RAF LYSANDER RESCUES WOUNDED AMERICAN OFFICER FROM THE BALKANS'. An unarmed RAF Lysander aircraft, piloted by Fg Off H. Attenborrow of New Southgate, London, made a daring flight of over 500 miles from an airfield in Southern Italy to pick up a severely wounded American officer at a Partisan landing strip in the heart of the German occupied Balkans. The American officer was in great pain from the severe wounds he had received as result of enemy action, and unless he received immediate expert medical attention, would only have lived for twelve hours. Well within the time limit, and for most of the dangerous journey unescorted, the Lysander removed the American officer and brought him safely back to an Italian airfield. Here, an ambulance, a doctor and a medical team were waiting and rushed him to a nearby hospital to receive expert treatment. (Original Caption, British Official Photograph No. CAN 3133 via author)
This epic rescue by Attenborrow was carried out by a 148 Squadron Lysander Mk IIIA in September 1944 from Brindisi. This diverse unit also operated the Halifax Mk II and V and Stirling Mk IV at the same time.

The Lysander also briefly saw a period of SD operations in the Far East when 357 Squadron added Mk IIIAs to its inventory in March 1945. The ex-161 Squadron aircraft were operated in Burma, from Meiktila, Don Muang and Mingaladon, in support of Force 136 and agents working behind the Japanese lines. However, the rough jungle airstrips and the Lysander's undercarriage were not a happy marriage, and at least four aircraft were wrecked by July 1945.

These 'Lizzies' were the last to see operational service during World War Two, and the few that survived the jungle strips remained the only ones that would still be operational in peacetime. Their service continued until 7 November 1945, when 357 Squadron was disbanded.

'SPECIAL DUTIES' UNITS AND THEIR AIRCRAFT

419 Flight
(Mk I) R2625, R2626; (Mk III) R9027

1419 Flight
(Mk III) T1508, T1770, T1508

138 Sqn
(Mk I) R2625, R2626; (Mk III) T1508, T1770, T1771

148 Sqn
(Mk I) R2640; (Mk III) T1672; (Mk IIIA) V9498, V9541, V9615; (Mk III TT) R9009, T1456, T1458, T1583, T1642, T1679, T1692, T1750; (Mk IIIA TT) V9670, V9707, V9816, V9821

161 Sqn
(Mk I) R2626; (Mk III) R9106 'K', P9129, R9125, T1503, T1770; (Mk IIIA) V9283, V9297, V9326, V9353, V9367, V9375, V9405 'B', V9428, V9490 'H', V9548 'D', V9595, V9597, V9614, V9664, V9673 'J', V9674 'K', V9718, V9723 'H', V9737, V9738, V9748 'D', V9749 'M', V9822 'E', V9858; (Mk III LR) R9117; (Mk III TT) T1446, T1651, T1688, T1707; (Mk III TT/SD) T1618

357 Sqn
(Mk III) V9295; (Mk IIIA) V9303, V9512, V9649, V9665; (Mk III TT) T1532, T1688; (Mk IIIA TT) V9289, V9494, V9495, V9808, V9815, V9818, V9867, V9885, V9889

The pilot of the Lysander has just returned from a reconnaissance flight and is making his report to the Air Intelligence Liaison Officer (AILO, on right). A despatch rider stands by, and a machine gunner keeps a look-out for enemy aircraft. The mobile HQ on the right is equipped with a wireless by means of which it keeps in touch with aircraft whilst on patrol. (Via Martyn Chorlton)

Chapter 6

Towing the Line

Multi-variant target tug

During World War Two, Westland's Lysander saw service in a variety of guises, most of which – because of its performance limitations – ironically brought it into close contact with danger. Of these dangers, none could be more alarming for the crew than towing a target for some hot-shot fighter pilot to attempt to shoot it full of holes.

Although precise numbers are difficult to verify, it seems likely that almost 50 per cent of the total Lysander production of 1,650 (including those built in Canada) ended up as Target Towing (TT) versions somewhere in the world. These included conversions of the relevant standard marks to TT Mk I, TT Mk II and TT Mk III, but the major variant was the TT Mk IIIA, of which 123 examples were conversions from the Mk III with further batches, amounting to 117 Lysanders, built from the outset as TT Mk IIIAs – as were almost all of the 225 examples built in Canada. In general, the Lysander TT versions saw service between 1942 and 1944 as far afield as Canada, Great Britain and India, until, in their turn, they were replaced by towing aircraft that were more in tune with the faster speeds of operational fighter aircraft. Lifting the lid on the wartime Central Gunnery School (CGS) provides us with a brief insight into the Lysander's target-towing role.

Lysander TT Mk III, R9003, of 7 AGS (Air Gunnery School) towing a drogue off Porthcawl, as viewed from one of the unit's many Avro Ansons. (*Aeroplane*)

The Central Gunnery School

On 1 April 1942, CGS moved in to Sutton Bridge and inherited four Lysander TTs from the previous occupant; 56 OTU, a Hawker Hurricane OTU that also used target-towing aircraft. Prior to April 1942, this facility was provided variously by Fairey Battle TT, Hawker Henley and Westland Lysanders of 1489 Target Towing Flight, formerly known as Sutton Bridge Station Flight, which was kept very busy by the Hurricane OTU 'tyros' and aircraft from operational fighter squadrons visiting the Holbeach Marsh Range for air gunnery practice. Sutton Bridge Station Flight had been redesignated 1489 Flight during September 1941, but when CGS arrived in April 1942 a cadre of 1489 Flight moved out to RAF Matlaske, leaving behind four Lysanders with which CGS began to operate its own integral Target Towing Flight. This number was rapidly increased to around ten aircraft, nine of which have been positively identified: T1429, T1444, T1459, T1618, all Mark III conversions to TT Mk III; V9496, a Mk IIIA converted to TT Mk IIIA; V9813, V9822, V9901 and W6955, built as TT Mk IIIAs. The CGS chief instructor complained to his superiors that the ideal establishment ought to have been closer to 18, but this was never achieved while at Sutton Bridge.

'…tell 'em I'm pulling it, not pushing it!'

The Lysander was a responsive and manoeuvrable aircraft with an ample 'girth' in the rear cockpit area that made it ideal for a winch. The IIIA was modified for target towing by mounting an electrically cranked, three-drum winch between the pilot and observer positions, in a way that still allowed space beneath the rear canopy for an operator to manipulate access doors, the winch, cable and targets.

The penultimate Lysander TT Mk IIIA to leave the Westland production line was V9905, seen at Yeovil in December 1941. Just visible are the black and yellow undersides, the towing cable guide to the rear of the undercarriage and the towing gear and winch mounted above the fuel tank between the pilot and observer. (Via Martyn Chorlton)

The winch drums contained enough wire cable to allow a target to be streamed out to about 1,000 to 1,200ft astern of the tug. Running the risk of lacerations or worse, winch operators were forbidden to handle the cable unless they wore heavy duty protective gloves. A pair of doors were built into the floor of the observer area to allow the cable and targets to be let in and out while in the air. The doors could be lifted and opened inwards prior to streaming the cable. Just outside and slightly forward of the doors was a bracket with a reel, through which the tow cable was made to turn through 90 degrees to clear the floor aperture and the tail wheel. Further protective wires were secured around the fin, rudder and tailplane assembly to prevent the towing cable from interfering with the rear control surfaces.

The aircraft itself was usually painted in the prevailing camouflage pattern on upper surfaces, but in its towing role it was embellished with garish (but highly visible), three-feet wide black stripes, painted at a 60-degree angle at 6ft intervals over a 'trainer' yellow on the under-surface of the wings. Some aircraft are known to have had a broad yellow band around the wheel spats and rear fuselage. Such visible markings, however, still did not prevent some of the TT 'Lizzies' being 'shot up' from time to time, and winch operators – usually groundcrew airmen with no aircrew 'brevet' – certainly earned their one shilling and sixpence (£2.97 in 2012) a day flying pay (danger money?). There is an apocryphal story doing the rounds to the effect that, on one such hairy occasion, an unknown pilot yelled at his winch operator to 'tell 'em I'm pulling it, not pushing it!'.

Red, blue and green

At CGS, all the air firing sorties were carefully briefed and closely controlled by air-to-air and air-to-ground radio, and the chief instructor was in direct contact with the Range by landline telephone. Fighter pilot students from the Pilot Gunnery Instructor Wing performed their 'live' shooting at towed drogues out over The Wash and its marshes. A 'sleeve' drogue was most commonly used since its 'wind-sock' shape, which inflated as air passed rapidly and constantly through it, gave the impression of a 'fuselage' as a fighter came in to attack. A Lysander could carry three or four of these target drogues – made from canvas, measuring 20ft in length, 4ft in diameter at the mouth and tapering to 2ft at the tail. The 'mouth' was kept open by a substantial piece of wood across the diameter, and a pear-shaped lead weight of about 5lb was secured to the lower edge of the mouth to help keep the drogue stable in flight. Usually, three fighter students would shoot at one drogue on each gunnery sortie. The 'ball' heads of the ammunition loaded into their Spitfires were dipped in a non-drying paint, with a different colour for each student – usually red, green or blue. When the drogue was examined after a firing exercise, the coloured edges of any shot holes in the drogue identified which student had fired the shots.

Every 'shoot' by each student was carefully recorded, and results were plotted in tabular and graph form, so that instructors and students could see how performance fluctuated; generally speaking – under the intensive and strict training regime – they all showed steady improvement. It was said that it was quite usual to find some students arriving at CGS with something of a reputation as a 'hot shot', but few of them shone in their first few encounters with a target drogue.

CGS scoring methods during 1943 were as follows. A drogue was divided into three sections, although this was purely notional since no delineation was marked on the actual target itself. Hits on part 'A', closest to the 'mouth' where the cable was attached – about one sixth of the total length – counted highest because this section represented the most vulnerable components of an enemy aircraft: pilot, engine and fuel tanks for example. The remainder of the drogue was divided into two equal parts, 'B' and 'C'. There were two sets of points that could be awarded depending on the type of exercise being flown. Against 'bombers', one point was given for hits in 'A' and half a point for hits in 'B' and 'C'. Against 'fighters', 'A' and 'B' were regarded as the vulnerable forward area, and hits in those areas counted for three points, while hits in area 'C' counted as half a point.

Since judgment of size and distance in the air was always the tricky issue for fighter pilots, in order to prepare students for the way a real drogue would look at the correct firing distance in the air, a 1:12 scale model was set up on the ground. They could practise ranging this through a standard reflector sight, as is fitted to current fighters.

Streaming out

While CGS was at Sutton Bridge, the bleak Holbeach Marsh Range continued to provide the air space and ground targets for air-to-air, air-to-ground and low-level strafing practice. During most of their working days, Lysanders were detached to the Holbeach Range landing ground and were flown to and from there at the beginning and end of the working day. This landing ground was a small grass field at the end of Durham's Road, adjacent to the Range Administration and Domestic site that was tucked up against the landward side of the sea bank at Gedney Dawsmere, and from which it took no time at all to fly onto station to begin a towing sortie over the Range. Targets were also marked here, and results telephoned back to Sutton Bridge so that they were available almost as soon as the students had landed. In order to maximize airtime productivity of the target tugs, and thereby increase the air firing time available to gunnery students, three or four targets were carried aboard the tug. This meant that when one exercise was completed, the 'used' target could be wound in, disconnected and dropped from the Lysander during a low, slow pass over the landing ground, where it would be marked and repaired, while the airborne winch operator readied the next target for streaming out for another batch of fighters over the Range.

Norman 'Taff' Warren found himself posted to the wilds of CGS Sutton Bridge, but he and many of his compatriots were soon moved out of the Station and billeted in the village. He was not sure whether this was a safety measure as a direct result of the bombing raids or the result of the influx of the

Originally built as a Mk III this Lysander, T1444, was converted to TT Mk III standard before it entered RAF service. The aircraft went on to only serve with 5 AOS (Air Observers School) based at Jurby on the Isle of Man, where the aircraft is flying just off the coast. (Alastair Goodrum)

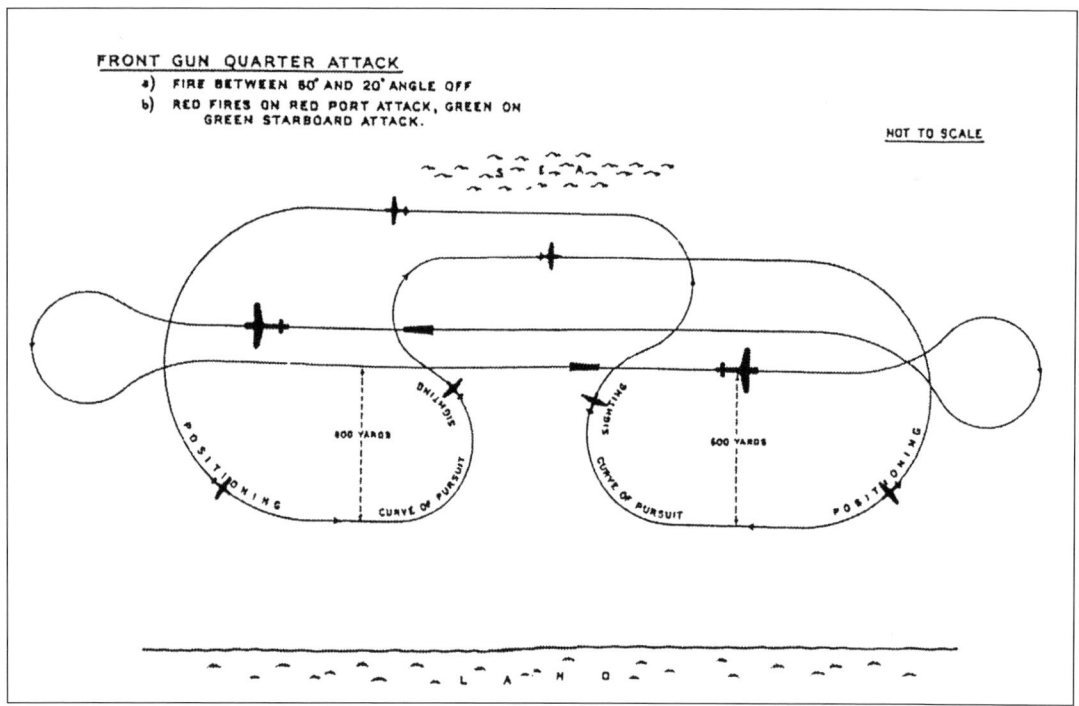

A diagram from instructional material used in the Pilot Gunnery Instructor course at Central Gunnery School while located at Sutton Bridge. The 'Land' represents the bank at Gedney Drove End and the 'Sea', in this case, would be The Wash. During this quarter attack exercise, towing aircraft travel parallel to the land and attacking fighters fire out to sea. (Alastair Goodrum)

Women's Auxiliary Air Force (WAAF) – but he thought it more likely the latter. He had the pleasure of staying with Mrs Sage in Custom House Street, about a half a mile walk from the camp. Widow of the former railway station master, Mrs Sage had Taff and one other airman under her roof and received the sum of six shillings a week (£11 in 2012) from the RAF for doing so. Inevitably, the airmen and WAAFs quickly got on good terms, and Taff Warren was no exception. He worked as a fitter on 'C' Flight, servicing Lysander target tugs and met his future wife at Sutton Bridge airfield, where she worked as an armourer; the station armoury being located adjacent to 'C' Flight dispersal. Taff also recalled flying down to the Range landing strip in the mornings, performing minor servicing on the Lysanders between towing duties, then flying back to Sutton Bridge when the day's towing was over. During her time at CGS Bomber Wing in 1942–43, Cpl (W) Olive Moule remembered 'seeing a Lysander parked in a special corner of the perimeter track, which always had an air of mystery about it and we wondered if it was one of those that flew over to Holland or France at night'.

Slicing the cable

Records indicate that about 3 per cent of targets were shot away from their towing cable, which of course meant that an exercise had to be aborted so that the tug could recover what was left of the cable and return to base for appropriate repairs. On 3 March 1943, for example, Flt Lt Lance Burra-Robinson, a flying instructor from 41 OTU at Hawarden, who was on detachment to CGS as a gunnery student, had a nasty surprise while firing over the Range in Mustang Mk I AP170. Firing at a drogue, his rounds sliced it from the towing cable, and the Mustang flew into the wallowing canvas tube – weights and all – damaging one wing of the aircraft. He landed safely at Sutton Bridge, and he

Another view of TT Mk IIIA V9905, which went on to serve with 58 OTU based at Grangemouth and would most likely have been seen at the unit's satellite at Balado Bridge. The aircraft gave faultless service until it was SOC on 25 January 1944. (Via Martyn Chorlton)

clearly learned something from his CGS experiences since he finished the war as a squadron leader with a DFC and five kills to his name.

There was a narrow squeak for the youngsters of Dawsmere Primary School on 5 July 1942 too. Returning from a target-towing sortie in Lysander TT Mk III T1618, staff pilot Sgt W. M. L. Penny narrowly missed hitting the school when he had to force-land due to running out of petrol. This was followed on 17 July by Lysander TT Mk IIIA V9496, making a rough landing at Sutton Bridge, causing the normally resilient undercarriage to fold and the 'Lizzie' to collapse in a heap; luckily, the crew escaped with just cuts and bruises.

Incidents and accidents

The Range landing ground at Gedney Dawsmere was a 'pocket-handkerchief' affair, and though this would normally present no great difficulty for a Lysander, which could land on a sixpence, there were, nevertheless, a number of mishaps mostly caused by the tight landing area. On 11 May 1943, Flt Sgt W. S. Johnson was doing a circuit just after take-off in TT Mk IIIA, W6955, when there was a bang, and his cockpit began to fill with acrid smoke. The engine had suffered a big end failure, and he only just squeezed into the landing ground after the engine seized up. Sgt A. George overshot during a landing on 15 April, and he ran into a dyke. Flt Lt A. R. Dunn did a similar trick on 9 June, and ran his TT Mk IIIA, V9901, into the sea bank. On 26 July, TT Mk III T1459, flown by Flt Sgt R. P. Wilson, suffered a tail wheel oleo collapse on landing, but he was uninjured. Sgt H. Mantell, though, was not quite so lucky on 23 September. His Lysander TT Mk IIIA suffered engine failure at 800ft during a live firing sortie, and he could not make it back to the Range landing strip. Just managing to hop over the sea bank, he set it down in a potato field where it ran into a farm plough before coming to rest upside down in a dyke. He was slightly injured. Fenland dykes were one of the most effective 'stoppers', as Sgt T. J. Fogg found out when he overshot the Range landing ground in TT Mk IIIA W6955 on a cold December day in 1943.

It was quite normal to see the occasional Lysander from units other than CGS over The Wash, and the worst incident involving a TT Lysander actually occurred not to a CGS aeroplane but to one from 3 OTU based at RAF Cranwell. The origins of this particular incident on 21 January 1943 were back at RAF Digby, where 411 (Canadian) Squadron operated Spitfire VB fighters. That morning,

First formed at Driffield in North Yorkshire to serve 4 Group bomber units, 1484 (TT) Flight was equipped with up to a dozen Lysanders between late 1941 and early 1943. (Via Martyn Chorlton)

Built from new as a target tug TT Mk IIIA V9817 saw RAF service with 4 Gp AACF and 21 OTU before being transferred to the USAAF's 2025 Gunnery Flight on 10 March 1943. (Via Martyn Chorlton)

seven Spitfires from 'B' Flight were airborne at 1010hrs for a flight formation exercise, which was to be followed by test firing the cannon on each aircraft. The formation crossed the coast at Skegness, and the flight commander gave the 445 order for each pilot to break away, with a wing-man accompanying him, according to a pre-arranged plan. That plan required each pilot in turn to dive towards the sea and fire his cannon into the water then climb to rejoin the formation. Meanwhile, Lysander TT Mk IIIA V9797 from 3 OTU, flown by WO William Atkins, with an unidentified winch operator in the back, was trundling over Wainfleet Range in The Wash, towing a target in the designated area.

Having served with 110 Squadron, Royal Canadian Air Force, as a MK III, R9003 was converted into a target tug to serve with 2 AOS and 7 AGS. (Via Martyn Chorlton)

The Lysander was heavily employed across the Commonwealth as a target tug, a role it performed in large numbers from 1941 to 1943, by which time more specialist types such as the Miles Martinet were being brought into service. (*Aeroplane*)

The 'Lizzie' was hit by Spitfire AA754 flown by WO John McMillan, RCAF, who was accompanying another Spitfire on its way down. Disintegrating as they fell, the Lysander and Spitfire plunged into The Wash two miles south of Skegness and about 100 yards offshore. The Canadian formation circled the area until an All Surface Rescue (ASR) boat reached the scene, but no survivors were found. Two bodies, those of Atkins and McMillan, were later recovered from the sea by the Skegness lifeboat, but the winch operator was never found.

SPECIALIST RAF LYSANDER TT UNITS

1 Gp (TT) Flt: Formed 18 September 1941 at Goxhill with 9+3* Lysanders; to Binbrook, 10 November 1941. Redesignated 1481 (TT) Flt, 14 November 1941.

2 Gp (TT) Flt: Reformed 30 September 1941 at West Raynham with 6+2 Lysander TTs; redesignated 1482 TT Flt.

3 Gp (TT) Flt: Formed at Marham on 14 February 1940 from a 98 Squadron detachment that had been operating a TT service using Battles from Mildenhall, Catfoss and Waddington since October 1939. It is not clear when Lysanders complemented Battles in the role. Redesignated as 1483 TTF on 18 November 1941.

4 Gp (TT) Flt: Formed at Driffield on February 1940 from Linton-on-Ouse Station Flight, which had been operating 2+1 Battles towing targets for 4 Gp Whitley squadrons. Again unclear when Lysanders complemented Battles. Operated from Cottam between 29 September and 24 October 1940, following a very heavy raid on Driffield. Amalgamated with 5 Gp TTF at Driffield until 2 April 1941 with 13+2 Battle (no mention of Lysander); Cottam again from 12 May 1941 to 28 September 1941. Redesignated 1484 TTF on 14 November 1941.

5 Gp (TT) Flt: From October 1939 at Finningley, to provide towed targets for 5 Gp Hampden squadrons using 2+1 Battles; TT detachment maintained at Catfoss and later Waddington; 5 Gp TTF formed 14 February 1940 at Driffield but amalgamated with 4 Gp TTF on 2 April 1941 with 13+32 Battles. To Coningsby 2 April 1941; detached to Scampton 19 August to 2 October 1941. Disbanded into 1485 TTF on 14 November 1941.

6 Gp (TT) Flt: Formed at Abingdon on 27 December 1939 to tow targets for 6 Gp squadrons. From 6 March 1940 tasking taken over by Bicester Station Flight. Arrangement ended February 1941, when OTUs took over.

9 Gp (TT) Flt: Formed at Valley on 16 July 1941 with an establishment of 3+1 Lysander. Redesignated as 1486 TTF on 8 December 1941.

10 Gp (TT) Flt: Formed at Warmwell on 16 July 1941 with 6 Lysanders. To Filton October 1941; to Warmwell November 1941. Redesignated as 1487 TTF on 8 December 1941.

11 Gp (TT) Flt: Formed at Shoreham on 16 July 1941 with an establishment of 7+3 Lysanders. To Ford in October 1941; to Shoreham 25 October 1941. Redesignated 1488 TTF on 1 December 1941.

12 Gp (TT) Flt: Formed at Coltishall on 16 July 1941 with an establishment of 4+2 Lysanders. To Sutton Bridge on 2 October 1941. To Matlask on 13 April 1942. Redesignated 1489 TTF on 8 December 1941.

13 Gp (TT) Flt: Formed at Acklington on 16 July 1941 with establishment of 4+1 Lysanders. Redesignated 1490 TTF on 8 December 1941.

14 Gp (TT) Flt: Formed at Inverness/Longman in October 1941 with an establishment of 4+1 Lysanders. Redesignated 1491 TTF on 8 December 1941.

82 Gp (TT) Flt: Formed at Ballyhalbert on 2 November 1941 with 2+1 Lysander TTs. Redesignated 1480 TTF on 24 November 1941.

1481 (TT) Flt: Formed 14 November 1941 (ex-No.1 Gp TTF) at Binbrook with 12 Lysanders for gunnery co-operation with 1 Gp units. Redesignated as 1481 Target Towing and Gunnery Flight (TTGF) in January 1942; Lysanders replaced by Martinets in February 1943.

1482 (TT) Flt: Formed November 1941 from 2 Gp TTF at West Raynham, initially with 6+2 Lysanders and 4 Blenheims for gunnery co-operation with 2 Gp units. Redesignated 1482 TTGF in January 1942. Renamed 1482 (Bomber) Gunnery Flight on 2 May 1942; Lysander replaced by Martinet from January 1943 onwards.

1483 (TT) Flt: Formed 18 November 1941 from 3 Gp TTF at Newmarket, initially with Lysanders and Wellingtons to provide air gunner refresher training for 3 Gp units. Redesignated as 1483 TTGF with 9+3 Lysanders on 7 February 1942. Became 1483 (Bomber) Gunnery Flight in July 1942. From July 1943, Lysanders replaced with Martinets.

1484 (TT) Flt: Formed 14 November 1941 from 4 Gp TTF at Driffield, initially with Lysanders and Battles to provide air gunner refresher training for 4 Gp units. Redesignated 1484 TTGF with 9+3 Lysanders. Became 1484 (Bomber) Gunnery Flight in May 1942; Lysander not mentioned in establishment for February 1943.

1485 (TT) Flt: Formed 30 October 1941 at Coningsby with 9+3 Lysanders to provide air gunner refresher training for 5 Gp units; 7 January 1942 absorbed 5 Gp TTF and redesignated 1485 TTGF; April 1942 establishment 8 Whitley and 9+3 Lysanders. Became 1485 (Bomber) Gunnery Flight; Target-towing detachment at Coningsby from 1 August 1942 to 8 March 1943. To Fulbeck on 27 October 1942. Became 1485 (Bombing) Gunnery Flight; February 1943 establishment still included 4 Lysanders; Martinets by August 1943.

1486 (TT) Flt: Formed on 30 October 1941 from 9 Gp TTF at Valley, initially with 3+1 Lysanders to provide gunnery refresher training for 9 Gp units; 22 April 1942 became 1486 (Fighter) Gunnery Flight; 7 October 1942 establishment included 4 Lysanders. To Llanbedr 8 July 1943. Disbanded into 12 APC on 18 October 1943.

1487 (TT) Flt: Formed 30 October 1941 from 10 Gp TTF at Warmwell, initially with 4+2 Lysanders to provide air gunnery refresher training to 10 Gp units (dets to Portreath January 1942 to June 1942, Fairwood Common from 4 April 1942 to 13 September 1943, Exeter from 2 October 1942 to August 1943 and Colerne from 1 March 1943 to 31 July 1943). Became 1487 (Fighter) Gunnery Flight 22 April 1942; July 1942 carried out target towing for United States Army Air Force P-38 units; 7 October 1942 establishment included 7+2 Lysanders. To Fairwood Common 13 September 1943. Disbanded into 11 APC on 18 October 1943.

1488 (TT) Flt: Formed 1 December 1941 from 11 Gp TTF at Shoreham, initially with 7+3 Lysanders to provide air gunnery refresher training for 11 Gp units. To Rochford 9 February 1943; 3 March 1942 Lysanders increased to 12+2; 29 April 1942 No.1 Flight to Shoreham and No.2 Flight to Rochford; 22 April 1942 became 1488 (Fighter) Gunnery Flight; 7 June 1942 to

Martlesham Heath (dets to Ipswich 7 October 1942 and Ford from 1 February 1943); 17 August 1943 to Southend. Disbanded into 17 APC on 18 October 1943, by which time Lysanders may have been fully replaced by Martinets.

1489 (TT) Flt: Formed 8 December 1941 from 12 Gp TTF at Coltishall, initially with 4+2 Lysanders and Henleys to provide air gunnery refresher training for 12 Gp units; 22 April 1942 became 1489 (Fighter) Gunnery Flight (dets to East Fortune from 13 September 1942, High Ercall December 1942 to June 1943, Kirton-in-Lindsey from December 1942 to April 1943 and Ludham from December 1942 to 1943); 30 March 1942 7+2 Lysanders on strength. To Matlask 13 April 1942; 2 June 1943 to Hutton Cranswick to operate in conjunction with 1495 Flight (det Catterick from July 1943). Disbanded into 16 APC on 18 October 1943.

1490 (TT) Flt: Formed 8 December 1941 from 13 Gp TTF at Acklington with 4+1 Lysanders and Henleys to provide air gunnery refresher training for 13 Gp units; 22 April 1942 became 1490 (Fighter) Gunnery Flight; 1942 re-equipped with Masters and Martinets, although 7 Lysanders were still on strength in February 1943.

1491 (TT) Flt: Formed 8 December 1942 from 14 Gp TTF at Inverness, initially with 3+1 Lysanders to provide air gunnery refresher training for 14 Gp units. To Tain 26 December 1941; 22 April 1942 became 1490 (Fighter) Gunnery Flight. To Skaebrae 15 November 1942. To Castletown 16 August 1943 to Peterhead October 1943 with 5+2 Lysanders on strength. Disbanded into 15 APC 18 October 1943.

1492 (TT) Flt: Formed 18 October 1941 in 70 Gp at Weston Zoyland, initially with 4+1 Lysanders to assist in the operation of Lilstock firing range; 22 April 1942 became 1492 (Fighter) Gunnery Flight; Master and Martinet progressively added through 1942 and no Lysanders on strength by early 1943.

1493 (TT) Flt: Formed 31 Oct, 1941 ex-83 Gp TTF at Ballyhalbert, initially with 2+1 Lysander TTs to provide air gunnery refresher training for 82 Gp units; to Newtownards 6 January 1942 (dets Eglinton March 1942 to 23 August 1942, Ballyhalbert 6 April 1942 to 26 January 1943 and Kirkistown 6 April 1942 to November 1942); 22 April 1942 became 1493 (Fighter) Gunnery Flight. To Ballyhalbert 26 January 1943. To Eastchurch 14 April 1943 as a lodger with 54 Gp (det Westhampnett 9 June 1943 to 1 July 1943). To Detling 26 July 1943 and 11 Gp control. To Gravesend 7 October 1943. Disbanded into 18 APC on 18 October 1943.

1494 (TT) Flt: Formed 18 December 1941 at Long Kesh, initially with Lysanders to provide air gunnery refresher training for RAF Northern Ireland units. To Sydenham 13 April 1942. To Ballyhalbert 16 April 1943. To North Weald 5 March 1945; Masters only added in May 1945. Disbanded 30 June 1945.

1495 (TT) Flt: Formed 8 August 1942 at Sawbridgeworth (34 Wing) with 3+1 Lysanders to provide TT facilities for the air-to-ground range at Mersea Island. To Hutton Cranswick 10 July 1943 and 12 Gp control. Disbanded into 16 APC on 14 November 1943.

1496 (TT) Flt: Was to form on 11 November 1942 at Hawarden with 4+2 Lysanders but 41 and 42 OTUs received 3+1 Lysanders each instead.

1497 (TT) Flt: Formed 8 March 1943 at Macmerry (33 Wing) with 3+1 Lysanders to provide air gunnery refresher training for local units. To Ayr 22 June 1943; To Shoreham 3 July 1943 under 11 Gp control. Disbanded into 17 APC on 18 October 1943.

1498 (TT) Flt: Formed 8 March 1943 at Hurn (38 Wing) with 3+1 Lysanders to provide air gunnery refresher training for 10 Gp units. To Colerne 14 August 1943. To Fairwood Common 12 September 1943. Disbanded 18 October 1943 into 11 APC.

1500 (TT) Flt: Formed 4 May 1943 at North Front to provide target facilities for RAF units based at Gibraltar, initially equipped with Lysanders but these were replaced by Martinets by March 1944.

The following, which were not solely target-towing units, also employed the Lysander for this duty

1, 2, 3, 4, 7, 8, 9, 10 and 13 AGS; 1 AGS (India); 1, 2, 4, 5 and 9 AOS; 1, 2, 3, 4, 11 and 16 APC.

*The unit's establishment is expressed, for example as 9+3; the former number is the initial establishment of the unit and the latter the immediate reserve.

'Interpretation Staff at Work'. An army co-op aircraft has returned from a photographic reconnaissance, and the prints are now in the hands of the interpretation staff. With the aid of stereoscopic and other viewing devices, they are able to gather valuable and highly accurate information regarding the disposition of enemy troops upon which the army commander will base his future campaign. (Via Martyn Chorlton)

Chapter 7

Re-Equipping the Eastern Tiger

Reluctant modernisation

The first Lysander to arrive in India was the second prototype, K6128, which was shipped to Karachi in March 1938 for tropical flight trials. RAF Lysander units, such as 20 and 28 squadrons, would also see service in India, but in 1939 all eyes were turning to the forthcoming war in Europe. The RAF needed every unit it could muster and to release squadrons, the manpower-consuming task of patrolling the northwest frontier was being prepared for transfer to the IAF. (At this stage of World War Two, no consideration was given to Japan joining the conflict, let alone being on the side of the Axis powers.) At this time, many did not think that the IAF, which at the time was operating the Hawker Audax and Hart with no sign of a replacement, was up to the task. Clearly, the IAF needed to go through a period

Originally formed in 1933, 1 Squadron is the oldest Indian Air Force (IAF) flying unit and still exists today (currently flying the Mirage 2000). It re-equipped with Lysanders in 1941 and all were emblazoned with the unit's tiger motif. 'Konkan' is a region on the West India coast. (Via *Aeroplane*)

of modernisation, but once again doubts were expressed that it would be able to cope with 'modern' aircraft such as the Westland Lysander.

By 1941, the decision was finally made to re-equip 1 (Indian) Squadron, under the command of Sqn Ldr S. Mukerjee, with the Lysander. Forty-eight Lysanders were allocated and delivered to the RAF depot at Drigh Road, which was also the home of the IAF's main aircraft depot. In August 1941, 1 Squadron was withdrawn from its duties on the northwest frontier to convert onto the Lysander under the guidance of the RAF. By September, all units operating along the frontier were being prepared for service in Europe, which forced 1 Squadron to return to Peshawar. One flight had to be left behind to complete its conversion training while the rest of the unit began a 750-mile flight northward with its new aircraft. Very conscious of the fact that the squadron was not deemed ready for its new charges, every effort was made to get all of the Lysanders to Peshawar without incident. This appeared in doubt when one of the machines damaged its undercarriage at Multan en route, but groundcrew, who were carried in the rear cockpits, effected a good repair, and 1 Squadron arrived at Peshawar without further incident.

Official handover

Still on RAF charge, the dozen Lysanders of 1 Squadron were officially handed over during a formal ceremony at Peshawar on 7 November 1941 by the governor of Bombay. The transfer had been made possible because they had been purchased by money donated from the Bombay War Gifts Fund. Without delay, the unit's aircraft were heavily involved in a working up period with the Indian Army operating along the Frontier. This region was unforgiving to all military equipment, and it was inevitable that 1 Squadron would suffer some early casualties, beginning with Lysander Mk II P1694 on 13 November. Whilst landing at Manzai, the Lysander hit a boulder, which caused the aircraft to cartwheel and end up in a heap of twisted wreckage, luckily without injury to the pilot. Only nine days later, a second aircraft was wrecked when it landed tail low at Lahore.

Increased strength

A second IAF unit, 2 (Indian) Squadron, which was initially formed with Audaxes, began to re-equip with the Lysander Mk I and Mk II from November 1941. The long-term plan was to raise a total of ten Indian squadrons, the third comprising Harts and Audaxes relinquished by 1 and 2 squadrons while 4 (Indian) Squadron began to receive the Lysander Mk I and Mk II from February 1942. To encourage international support and help recruit Indians to join their own air force, it was decided that 1 (Indian) Squadron, which was now fully equipped with 'modern' Lysanders, should be used to publicise the expansion. Part of this exercise involved several of the unit's Lysanders flying from Peshawar to Calcutta as part of the city's 'War Weapons Week'.

1 (Indian) Squadron left Peshawar on 29 November under the command of Sqn Ldr K. K. Majumdar, Sqn Ldr Mukerjee having been transferred to the Quetta Staff College. During the War Weapons Week, 1 (Indian) Squadron operated from Dum Dum, which was the home of 3 Coastal Defence Flight at the time. However, with only a few demonstration flights under its belt, news came through about the Japanese attack on Pearl Harbor, followed on 9 December by the Japanese offensive at Kota Bahru in Malaya and the Tenasserim Peninsula in Burma. The following day, 1 (Indian) Squadron received orders to move to Burma.

War footing

Being detached so far away from its home airfield, an immediate move to Burma was impossible. Another factor which prevented 1 (Indian) Squadron from reaching a war footing was a total lack of air

The very first Lysander to land on Indian soil was the second prototype, K6128, seen here at Miranshah during tropical trials. (Owen Cooper)

gunners. The unit had only become operational for its duties along the frontier, and for this role there was no need for an air gunner as there was no aerial opposition. To rectify this, volunteers were called for to train as air gunners, and, following a good response, and a hurried training programme, the unit prepared to depart for Burma. Unfortunately, before the unit set out, it sustained its first casualties of World War Two when Lysander Mk II R1989 undershot its approach, struck an embankment (bund) and overturned on 20 December 1941.

In the meantime, the Japanese made huge advances through Burma with such success that military leaders predicted that India could be overrun. A dozen Lysanders of 1 (Indian) Squadron began the long journey to Burma in stages, finally reaching their operational war station at Toungoo on 1 February 1942. It was at Toungoo where the unit was reunited with 28 Squadron of the RAF, also flying Lysanders, which the Indians had relived of its frontier duties in mid-1940 at Miranshah.

Into action

On the night of 1 (Indian) Squadron's arrival, Japanese bombers attacked Toungoo, but all of the Indian Lysanders escaped unharmed, and only minor damage was suffered by 28 Squadron's machines. Sqn Ldr Majumdar suspected that the Japanese bombers were operating from Mae-Haugsaum in Siam, and he alone decided that it was already time to take the war back to enemy. On 3 February, Sqn Ldr Majumdar and his air gunner set out, with just two Brewster Buffaloes of 67 Squadron as escort, to bomb the airfield at Mae-Haugsaum. Carrying a pair of 250lb bombs, Majumdar flew low over the enemy airfield dropping one of his precious bombs directly onto the only hangar.

On 4 February, Majumdar repeated the feat, although this time the entire complement of 12 1 (Indian) Squadron Lysanders attacked as well. Further success was achieved with bombs dropped on a wireless station, and several Japanese aircraft were dispersed before the unconventional bomber force headed for home, although to avoid enemy fighter interception 1 Squadron headed for Heho instead, returning to Mae-Haugsaum the following day.

Continuous Japanese success in the region saw the RAF's and IAF's precious aircraft spread thinly over a very large area. 1 Squadron found its limited resources sliced in two; one detachment being directed to Lashio to support the Chinese 5th Army and the remainder send to Mingaladon in support of ground forces that were valiantly defending Rangoon. The Lysanders suffered on a daily basis whilst operating from poorly repaired landing grounds; undercarriage failures and seized tail wheels were a regular occurrence. The latter were particularly vulnerable to shimmying, seizing or even breaking off, and in several instances the ever-resourceful Indian groundcrews actually replaced the Lysanders tail wheels with wooden ones! Generally, though, it was up to the pilot and air gunner to perform their own maintenance as landing grounds became more and more remote.

The primary role of all Lysanders in the region was that of tactical reconnaissance, but it was impossible to stop both the IAF and RAF crews from conducting as many offensive operations as possible. Low-level bombing raids became a short-lived forte; the Lysanders being flown so low the jungle canopy provided extra camouflage in order to evade Japanese fighters. So desperate were the Allies in their attempt to stem the Japanese advance, a World War One tactic of throwing hand grenades from the rear cockpit was employed by the air gunners.

Withdrawal to India

Despite the efforts of the Lysander crews, the withdrawal back into India began all too soon from late February 1942 onwards. 1 (Indian) Squadron was withdrawn from the Mingaladon region to Magwe, where it was joined by the remnants of the Lashio-based machines on 5 March. On 7 March, the Japanese pushed towards Rangoon where Allied troops were turning defence into retreat by destroying all immovable military equipment so that it would not fall into enemy hands. However, two very valuable pieces of military hardware had been left at Magwe in the shape of two fully serviceable Hurricanes. Word filtered through to Sqn Ldr Majumdar, who, without hesitation, arranged for two of his Lysanders to fly to Magwe, with Hurricane pilots in the rear cockpits to collect the two stranded fighters. As the lonely duo approached Magwe, a Japanese aircraft flew over the airfield, but, luckily for the Lysanders, it turned out to be a reconnaissance machine photographing the airfield. Before the enemy aircraft could return to its home airfield to develop and print its film, the Lysanders had landed and delivered their two Hurricane pilots, who quickly took off in the two fighters to escort the IAF aircraft back to Magwe.

Located behind a very dense stretch of jungle, Magwe's location gave the IAF and RAF time to recover their forces while the Japanese advance slowed to a snail's pace. By 12 March, 1 (Indian) Squadron only had four serviceable Lysanders on strength, and these were handed over to the Burmese Communications Flight to undertake evacuation work. All of 1 (Indian) Squadron's pilots were returned to India aboard one of the first B-17s in theatre, while they pondered what equipment could possibly replace their beloved Lysanders. 1 (Indian) Squadron's efforts had not gone unnoticed, and, for his outstanding leadership, Sqn Ldr Majumdar was awarded the DFC, while WO Harjinder Singh, the SNCO in charge of all ground maintenance, was deservedly awarded the MBE. Once safely back at Peshawar, the unit was reformed and re-equipped with the Hurricane – without a single doubt being expressed by any senior member of staff about how well the Indians would cope with such 'modern' equipment.

Tribal troubles

While 1 (Indian) Squadron converted to the Hurricane, 4 (Indian) Squadron was being formed at Peshawar with the Lysander Mk I and Mk II under the command of Flt Lt H. U. Khan. Its first batch of four Lysanders arrived on 16 February 1942, but the unit was not given much time to work up before its first task was issued. Four aircraft were detached to Kohat for operations along the frontier because local tribesmen had taken advantage of the idea that Japan could invade the south-eastern corner of India. The tribesmen had anticipated that India would reduce its ground forces along the frontier and, therefore, plundering attacks across the north-western plains could be undertaken relatively un-harassed by the Indian Army. These ideas were quickly quelled, when 4 (Indian) Squadron Lysanders, operating from Miranshah, conducted bombing operations against the tribesmen in the Sharani region. The Central Indian Hur tribe also began rioting, but this was soon controlled after a detachment of Lysanders were sent to Hyderabad.

By late 1942, the Lysanders of 4 (Indian) Squadron were performing army co-operation duties in support of the 7th Indian Division in the Risalpur region, but by this stage this tasking began to dwindle. The days of the Lysander in squadron service, both with the IAF and RAF, were numbered in India, as 2 and 4 (Indian) squadrons and the RAF's 20 and 28 squadrons converted to the Hurricane.

This was certainly not the end for the Lysander in India, which was still needed for target-towing duties, special supply operations along the Burmese Front and general communication duties. Lysander Mk IIIs and Mk IIIAs were also shipped to India for these roles, and a few of the latter did see service with 2 and 4 (Indian) squadrons. Many remained active until the end of World War Two in India.

The Lysander had once again proved that in determined hands it could be a useful aircraft, but just as in France, its primary role as a reconnaissance machine in India was not its strongest one.

One RAF unit which worked side by side with the Indian Air Force was 28 Squadron, reforming in India on 1 April 1920 with the F.2b. It operated the Lysander Mk II from September 1941 to December 1942 and was destined to remain in India and the Far East until 1978. (Owen Cooper)

LYSANDERS CREDITED IN INDIAN AIR FORCE SERVICE

(Mk I) P1674; P1675 (1 and 4 Sqn) Crashed in forced landing 70m NE of Hyderabad, 24 March 1943; P1677; P1690; P1694 (1 Sqn) Crashed on landing at Manzai after striking a boulder and cartwheeling, 13 November 1941; P1696; (Mk II) L4740 (2 Sqn); L4748 (2 Sqn) Bomb collapsed in forced landing 1m N of Golden North, Tamil Nadu, 14 September 1942; L4780 (2 Sqn); L4786 (4 Sqn); L4794 (4 Sqn) Lost height in valley and flew into hill near Datta Khei, DBF, 12 May 1942; L4797; L4798; L4801 (4 Sqn); L4815 (2 Sqn); L4816 (4 Sqn); N1209 (2 Sqn); N1212 (1 Sqn); N1224 (4 Sqn); N1242 (4 Sqn); N1255 (2 Sqn); N1256 (4 Sqn) Engine cut after t/o, dived into ground 5m NNW of Kohat, 20 March 1942; N1269 (4 Sqn); N1295 (4 Sqn); N1299 (2 Sqn); N1315 (1 AACU IAF); N1318 (2 Sqn); P1723; P1742; P9062; P9095; P9120; P9121 (4 Sqn); P9131 (4 Sqn); P9132; P9176 (2 Sqn); P9177 (4 Sqn); P9194 (2 Sqn) Undershot landing and tail knocked off; overturned, Yeravda, 28 March 1942; R1989 (1 Sqn) Undershot landing, hit bund and overturned in Peshawar, 20 December 1941; R2004 (4 Sqn); R2006 (4 Sqn); R2007 (1 and 2 Sqn); R2029; R2033 (1 Sqn) Swung on landing and the undercarriage collapsed, Peshawar, 16 January 1942; (Mk IIIA) V9308; V9325; V9384; V9427; V9440; V9718 and V9738.

INDIAN AIR FORCE LYSANDER UNITS

1 Sqn   *Ittehad Men Shakti Hai (Strength in Unity)*
A/c   Mk I and II, August 1941 to December 1942
Bases   Ambala, Peshawar, Dum Dum, Toungoo, Lashio, Mingaladon, Magwe

2 Sqn   *Amogh Lakshya (Unwavering Aim)*
A/c   Mk I and II, November 1941 to December 1942

4 Sqn   *Maan Par Jaan (Honour unto Death)*
A/c   Mk I and II, February 1942 to June 1943
Bases   Peshawar, Kohat, Miranshah, Hyderabad

Chapter 8

The 'Lizzie' and the 'Salvation Navy'

Air-sea rescue

For the first year of the war, the task of ASR was the responsibility of the station from which the missing aircraft was operating from. It was a completely uncoordinated service, and it was not until the enemy began to place a chain of rescue rafts in the Channel and operate specialised rescue floatplanes that the RAF realised it needed a dedicated service.

During the early stages of the Battle of Britain alone, at least 225 RAF aircrew had been lost at sea. By the end of July 1940, the CO of 11 Group, AVM K. R. Park, made an agreement with the army

RAF groundcrew pack an 'M' Type dinghy, which will be carried in the Small Bomb Container under the stub wing of the Lysander. Note the Walrus warming through its Pegasus engine in the background; all of the RAF's official Air-Sea Rescue (ASR) squadrons operated both types together at first. (*Aeroplane*)

co-operation wings to allocate 12 Lysanders for 'off-shore searching' duties. It was not until 22 August that the 'borrowed' Lysanders were officially placed under the control of Fighter Command. They were utilised for sea searches up to 20 miles offshore, covering the English coastline from the Wash to the Bristol Channel and the South Wales coast as far as Milford Haven.

The Lysander was incapable of carrying the standard Lindholme rescue gear, but, by early 1941, the aircraft had its own specifically designed equipment. It consisted of four small 'M' Type dinghies, distress flares, food and water all packed in a valise that could be fitted inside small bomb containers and carried under the stub wings.

Another six Lysanders had been added to Fighter Command's ASR network by May 1941, giving even greater coverage. This now ranged from the mouth of the Humber to the Isle of Man, and, to cover this vast area, two Lysanders were based at Coltishall, Exeter, Manston, Martlesham, Pembrey, Portreath, Shoreham, Tangmere and Warmwell. Expansion continued throughout 1941, and by

Groundcrew fit a dinghy rescue pack, specifically designed for the Lysander, to the starboard stub wing of a 277 (ASR) Squadron Lysander. Based at Stapleford Tawney, the squadron also operated detachments from Martlesham Heath, Shoreham and Tangmere. (Via Martyn Chorlton)

THE LYSANDER ASR FLIGHTS (UNITED KINGDOM)

Prior to the Lysander ASR squadrons being established, a rather confusing system of ten 'unnumbered' flights was authorised by the Air Ministry on 14 May 1941. Each flight was allocated two Lysanders, a dozen of which were acquired from 4, 13, 16, 225, 613 and 614 squadrons, while the remainder were drawn from storage. From June 1941, the number of Lysanders allocated to each 'flight' was raised to 2+1, and these were added to the following stations' establishments; 10 Group (Exeter, Pembrey, Portreath and Warmwell); 11 Group (Kenley, Manston, Martlesham Heath and Tangmere); and 12 Group (Coltishall).

The aircraft were eventually broken down into the following 'sections' (or the ten unnumbered flights), from which point they evolved into operational squadrons.

10 Group
1) Formed 14 May 1941 at Warmwell; became 'A' Flt, 276 Squadron, with 2+1 Lysanders on 21 October 1941.
2) Formed 14 May 1941 at Roborough; absorbed into 276 Squadron 21 October 1941.
3) Formed 14 May 1941 at Pembrey; to Fairwood Common 4 July 1941; became 'D' Flt, 276 Squadron, with 2+1 Lysanders on 21 October 1941.
4) Formed 18 July 1941 at Portreath with 2+0 Walruses; Became 'C' Flt, 276 Squadron, at Perranporth with 2+1 Lysanders and 1+0 Walrus on 11 November 1941. (276 Sqn HQ and 'B' Flt (2+1 Lysanders) were formed at Harrowbeer on 21 October 1941.

11 Group
5) Formed 14 May 1941 at Martlesham Heath (attached to 613 Squadron); became 'A', 277 Squadron, with 2+1 Lysanders on 22 December 1941.
6) Formed 18 July 1941 at Hawkinge with 2+0 Walruses; Became 'B' Flt, 277 Squadron, with 2+1 Lysanders and 1+0 Walrus on 22 December 1941.
7) Formed 14 May 1941 at Shoreham; to Freiston 9 July 1941; to Shoreham 15 October 1941; became 'C' Flt, 277 Squadron, with 2+1 Lysander on 22 December 1941.
8) Formed in 1941 at Merston; to Westhampnett on 15 November 1941; to Shoreham 30 November 1941 and absorbed into the Shoreham Flight.

12 Group
9) Formed July 1941 at Matlask; 2+0 Walrus added in August 1941; became 'A', 278 Squadron on 1 October 1941. This unit was (officially or unofficially?) referred to as 3 ASR Flight.
10) Formed 18 July 1941 at Coltishall with 2+0 Walrus; became part of 278 Squadron on 1 October 1941. (278 Sqn HQ formed at Matlask on 1 October 1941).

October the first of four specialised squadrons was formed. 275 Squadron at Valley, 276 Squadron at Harrowbeer and 278 Squadron at Matlask were all formed in October and 277 Squadron followed at Stapleford Tawney in December.

By now, 36 Lysanders were available across the country, making their presence felt to such an extent that they were nicknamed the 'Salvation Navy'. However, by 1942, a problem with spares was encountered as the type was out of production and large quantities of parts had been shipped to the Middle East and India where the Lysander was still operational. Fighter Command was forced to look for an alternative and in stepped the Defiant, of which there were plenty available following the introduction of the Beaufighter to the night fighter role. By mid-1942, the strength of the ASR squadrons had quickly turned, with the Defiant now the dominant type; by the year's end only four Lysanders remained on strength. By early 1943, the Lysander had served its purpose in another important role and was withdrawn.

THE LYSANDER ASR SQUADRONS

275 Squadron
Formed at Valley on 15, October 1941 with Lysander Mk I (1) and Mk III and Walrus. Detachments were undertaken at Andreas and Eglinton; Defiant Mk I added from May 1942 but gone by June 1943; Anson Mk I from March 1943 onwards; Lysander retired in September 1943.
   Aircraft: (Mk I) L4695; (Mk IIIA) V9405, V9737, V9738, V9739, V9748 and V9749.

276 Squadron
Formed at Harrowbeer on 21 October 1941 with Lysander Mk III and IIIA; Hurricane Mk I arrived in November 1941 and remained until January 1942; Walrus from January 1942. Detachments included Roborough, Portreath, Warmwell, Perranporth and Fairwood Common; Lysander retired in May 1943.
   Aircraft: (Mk III) T1620, T1621, T1696, T1698; (Mk IIIA) V9296, V9310, V9350, V9444, V9505, V9513, V9710, V9735 and V9743.

277 Squadron
Formed at Stapleford Tawney on 22 December 1941 with Lysander Mk IIIA and Walrus. Detachments to Martlesham Heath, Hawkinge and Shoreham; Defiant Mk I arrived in May 1942 but was withdrawn by May 1943. To Gravesend 7 December 1942 and further detachments to Hawkinge, Martlesham Heath and Shoreham; Spitfire Mk IIC arrived in February 1943 and served until May 1944. To Shoreham 15 April 1944 plus detachments to Martlesham Heath, Warmwell, Hurn and Hawkinge; Spitfire Mk VB arrived in April 1944; Lysander retired in June 1944.
   Aircraft: (Mk I) P1684; (Mk IIIA) V9364, V9402, V9431, V9445, V9473, V9483 (Engine failed, crash landed into trees and lost wing at Fosholt Farm, Kent on 16 April 1942), V9487**, V9488 (Overshot landing and hit fence at Hawkinge on 7 May 1942), V9545, V9547, V9583, V9588 and V9607.

278 Squadron
Formed at Matlask from 3 ASR Flight on 1 October 1941 with Lysander Mk IIIA and Walrus. Detachment to North Coates; To Coltishall 21 April 1942. Detachments to North Coates, Woolsington, Acklington, Hutton Cranswick, Ayr, Drem, Castletown, Peterhead and Sumburgh; Lysander replaced by Anson Mk I in February 1943.
   Aircraft: (Mk IIIA) V9297, V9369, V9538, V9541, V9609 and V9709.

**Served with 277 Squadron then transferred to 16 Squadron before returning to 277 Squadron.

Groundcrew of an unspecified ASR squadron mount a Mk VB Parachute Supply Dropper to the stub wing of a Westland Lysander. (*Topical Press* via *Aeroplane*)

A remarkable design solution for an anti-invasion aircraft, the prototype Lysander K6127 only spent a few months in the guise of the P.12 Wendover. The aircraft is pictured at Yeovil in July 1941. (Via Martyn Chorlton)

Lysander pilots and air gunners always took an active role in what and how the day's ordnance was loaded onto their aircraft's stub wings. The pilot in this case appears to be loading, or connecting the item on the port stub wing while his air gunner keeps a watchful eye over the armourers loading the starboard stub wing. (*Aeroplane*)

Chapter 9
The Ugly Ducklings

The coach-built P.12 Wendover

The prototype Lysander, K6127, was a hard-working aircraft that was subjected to several of the modifications within this article. The most striking was the installation of the Delanne-type tandem wing, combined with a Boulton-Paul rear turret (only a mock-up was ever fitted). Subjected to many names over the years, not all flattering, Westland designated the aircraft the P.12 Wendover, while in RAF circles it was generally known as the 'Tandem Wing' Lysander.

Converted in late 1940, the aircraft was designed to be used as an anti-invasion strafing aircraft, but as the Lysander's main armament was facing rearwards, the chances of it taking a large amount of fire from the ground was high, especially considering the speed the 'Lizzie' would be approaching at. The rear fuselage modification work was carried out by the coach-makers Harringtons of Hove, while the detailed design work was initiated at Yeovil. The standard wing was kept in situ, but to counteract the rear turret and generate more lift, a tailplane with large fins as endplates was installed. This still placed the centre of gravity (CoG) a lot further back than the original aircraft, but after being flight tested by Harald Penrose he reported that aircraft handled very well.

With the threat of an enemy invasion diminishing by the day, the Wendover did not arrive at the A&AEE at Boscombe Down until October 1941. The following is the official report on the trials of K6127 in its new guise.

Converted to the remarkable Delanne configuration in the summer of 1941, the prototype Lysander, K6127, was reconfigured back to its original layout by early 1942. Despite its ungainly appearance, the aircraft handled very well and was much appreciated by A&AEE test pilots. (Via Owen Cooper)

A&AEE Report No. 694; the Tandem Winged Lysander

The first prototype Lysander, K6127, was flown in June 1936 and was to have a much-photographed, long and colourful career, being sent pre-war to the northwest frontier of India for operational tests under active service conditions. That particular aircraft was to be the subject of A&AEE Report No. 694g and to become unique among the 1,368 Lysanders built.

Known as the Tandem Wing development, the prototype, K6127, was modified to take a wide span tailplane – virtually a second wing designed to the French Delanne formula – with twin endplate fins. That was not the extent of the modification, as Report 694 states: The fuselage was terminated by a mock-up of a Boulton-Paul four-gun (.303in) turret. The principle was merely an experiment to determine whether it was possible to provide really adequate rear defence on small aircraft without destroying the general flying characteristics.*

The second wing, which is what in reality the tailplane became, provided no less than 43 per cent of the net wing area. The size, and therefore lift, of this 'tailplane' was required because of the weight of the rear turret; its guns and gunner were at the maximum moment removed from the CoG datum. The CoG limits of this unique aircraft, from forward to aft, expressed as a percentage of the forward wings chord, were from 45.5 per cent to 58.2 per cent – a considerable range.

The brief performance tests began sometime in late January or early February 1942 (the report is dated 17 February), the first tentative ground taxiing trials being conducted below 40 mph. Handling was easy, but, above that speed, it was discovered that neither brakes nor full rudder could cope with keeping the

---

* While the A&AEE only viewed the aircraft as an experimental machine, Westland designed the Wendover with the hope of a large production order in mind.

One of a host of ideas for a dedicated anti-invasion aircraft, K6127 was modified with a new rear fuselage for a Boulton-Paul four-gun turret. While the design work was carried out at Yeovil, the actual work was handled by coachbuilders Harringtons of Hove. (Via Owen Cooper)

Lysander on course. Hardly surprisingly, in view of the weight aft, it was found that a full application of the wheel brakes produced no tendency for the aircraft to nose over, even with the CoG fully forward.

In spite of the marginal directional control, the take-off seems to have been normal, and the aircraft was reported as neutrally stable in the climb with the CoG aft. The twin rudders were light and effective, although the test pilot found them moderately heavy at 285mph in a dive.

The ability of the standard Lysander to fly slowly was always considered its main asset. The stalling speed is usually given as 65mph, but in fact the 'Lizzie', in the hands of a skilled pilot, could be trimmed into a stable, nose high, steep controlled stall, with the rate of descent determined by the throttle. It was possible, when in this condition, to continue to a perfectly satisfactory three-point landing, though pilots were warned that they might thus land safely in a field so small that to fly out of it could prove impossible.

The Tandem Wing rear turret modification does not seem materially to have compromised the ability of the Lysander to emulate if not a helicopter, certainly an autogyro: the A&AEE test pilots found that, even with the CoG at the maximum forward limit, the aircraft remained in level flight under full control with the stick right back, at the very low speed of 58mph – this at an all-up weight around 6,000lb. With the CoG aft, the testers noted a slight tendency for the wing to drop when the stick was brought right back at 60mph. Interestingly, the famed Lysander stalled stable glide could still be made (with the slats fully open) at 58mph. Conventional dives were reported

Officially designated as the P.12 Wendover, Westland had hoped that the aircraft would result in a substantial order from the Air Ministry. However, the anti-invasion role it was intended for had all but passed by the time the aircraft was being trialled at Boscombe Down. (Via Owen Cooper)

as 'smooth and remarkably steady'. With the CoG forward, the Lysander would, if trimmed for full throttle level flight, recover itself from a dive, hands off. At normal or aft CoG, however, the pilot had to initiate the recovery, though the stick force required was not excessive and recovery was positive and immediate.

The anti-invasion 'Pregnant Perch'

The slightly less well-known conversion of Lysander Mk I, L4673, into an anti-invasion aircraft was carried out when Britain had its back to the wall following the fall of France. It was nicknamed the 'Pregnant Perch' because of the expanded lower fuselage created for a new ventral gun position, enabling the gunner to fire downwards at troops or vehicles. Clearly not an attractive looking modification, hence the nickname, the project was cut short on 7 August 1940, when L4673 had to force-land after engine failure with Westland test pilot George Snarey at the controls. Snarey managed to escape unhurt, but L4673 was a write off.

Dive bomber

The Lysander was more than capable of attacking an opponent in a shallow dive, but could not be described as a dive-bomber. One aircraft, following the anti-invasion theme, was converted to this role, although the unknown Lysander was more likely used as a 'guinea pig' to trial a set of 'bench-type' airbrakes. Each airbrake was approximately 8ft long and 18ins deep and deployed from the underside of the wing. How effective they were is unknown, but a total of 24sq ft being pushed into the airflow must have slowed the aircraft considerably.

The demise of the 'Pregnant Perch'. The first production aircraft, L4637, was converted into another anti-invasion idea, which involved a ventral gun position for troop and beach strafing. In August 1940, test pilot George Snarey suffered an engine failure, but escaped unhurt after a challenging uphill crash landing under some HT cables. L4637 was written off, along with the idea. (Via Owen Cooper)

Although the Lysander was already designed to carry out dive-bombing, the concept was taken one step further when a pair of wing-mounted bench-type airbrakes were fitted to a single aircraft in 1940. It is most likely that the airbrakes were fitted for experimental rather than operational reasons. (Via Owen Cooper)

A Lysander with even more lift!

Lysander Mk II, P9105, an aircraft that had already spent a great deal of time with the RAE was selected to trial a new high-lift wing. Designed by aircraft structural engineer H. J. Steiger and built by the Blackburn Aircraft Company, the Blackburn-Steiger single-spar wing only had a span of 38ft and was swept forward by nine degrees. The wing had a parallel-chord, full span flaps and slats, and lateral control was initiated by wing tip spoilers. It is presumed that the wing worked well with the Lysander, but as it was only an experiment the aircraft reverted to its standard wing and served on until July 1943 with 516 Squadron.

Non-standard undercarriages

The ever-dutiful prototype, K6127, was called upon again during 1942 to trial two different kinds of undercarriage set-ups. The Lysander was already adept at getting in and out of small spaces, but Dowty thought it could make the aircraft even better by fitting a castoring main undercarriage. The idea was that the aircraft would be able to take-off or land into the wind, even if the runway was out of the wind! Obviously, crosswind landings are just one of many skills that should be in the repertoire of even the most average pilot, and the idea never materialised as an 'optional extra' on a future World War Two aircraft. Staying on the theme of small and rough landing grounds, K6127 was also trialled with a pair of caterpillar tracks instead of the main landing gear.

Not the most radical of Lysander modifications, the large bench-type airbrakes would clearly have radically slowed the aircraft whilst diving. (Via Owen Cooper)

Specifically for research purposes only, Lysander Mk II P9105 was fitted with a Blackburn-Steiger parallel-chord reduced span high-lift wing. It was fitted with full span flaps and slats and lateral control was achieved by wing tip spoilers. The wing only had a span of 38ft and a forward sweep of nine degrees. (Via Owen Cooper)

Defence and attack

One of the first non-standard armament trials once again involved K6127 and again followed an anti-invasion theme. During July 1940, K6127 was sent to the A&AEE sporting a pair of Oerlikon 20mm cannons mounted above each wheel fairing, firing outside of the arc of the propeller. Designed specifically for use against German invasion barges, the exposed cannons would have given the Lysander quite a forward-firing clout.

Another weapons proposal was to fit a Boulton-Paul Type 'A' Mk III turret in the observer's position. Armed with four .303in machine guns, the defensive capability of the aircraft would have been dramatically increased. The proposal only ever reached the mock-up stage, although a 'real' turret was fitted into the fuselage of Lysander Mk II P1723 for demonstration purposes.

Above: Swiss-born H. J. Steiger originally cut his designer teeth working for Beardmore and General Aircraft before moving to Blackburn to later become their chief designer. Steiger first applied for a patent for his wing designs in 1930 with Mr A. E. L. Chorlton and a Mr R. A. de Haig. (Via Owen Cooper)

Opposite above: Not long after the outbreak of the war the prototype, K6127 was fitted with a pair of Oerlikon 20mm cannons. They were fitted above the wheel fairings but were still just outside the arc of the propeller. Designed for attacking invasion barges, the idea was dropped by mid-1940. (Via Owen Cooper)

Opposite below: Another idea for giving the Lysander more firepower was the fitment of a four-gun power-operated turret, aft of the wing, in the position of the rear cockpit. Only reaching the mock-up stage, the idea was abandoned because the wing restricted the field of fire. (Via Owen Cooper)

Chapter 10

Builders of Transport for Canada

Hamilton production

During the late 1930s Canada began an extensive expansion programme of similar proportions to the RAF, which was bolstered by the mass production of several British aircraft designs including the Blenheim (aka Bolingbroke), Hurricane and the Lysander. Once the expansion period was over for Canada, the RCAF, which was a relative unknown during the 1930s, had grown to become the fourth largest air force in the world.

Production of the Lysander, at first, was somewhat conservative, with an order for just 28 Lysander Mk Is placed with the National Steel Car Corporation (NSCC) based in Hamilton, Ontario, in April 1938.

The NSCC had long built its reputation on the production of freight trucks and railway carriages, and in recent years had supported the fledgling Canadian aircraft industry by making steel panels and aluminium drop forgings. The NSCC's proud slogan was 'Builders of Transport for Canada', but this early order to build the Lysander saw the company quickly move from road and rail to the production of aircraft. Further orders were placed with the NSCC by the British government for 50 Lysander Mk Is, which was later increased to 150. The plan was to ship the Lysanders to Britain in component form, where they would be built by Westland and potentially Scottish Aviation, but none of the additional orders came to fruition as they were cancelled by the MAP in 1940.

Prior to the NSCC beginning production of the 28 Lysanders, the specification was altered from the Mercury engine to the Perseus, therefore the first Canadian-built machines were actually Mk IIs. These were built at NSCC's new factory at Malton, Ontario, and apart from a few metal panels being manufactured in a single piece, rather than two, the aircraft were identical to the Westland-built machine.

The National Steel Car Corporation of Canada licence-built 75 Lysander Mk IIs in the serial range 416 to 490. On the left, is one of the early aircraft, No.428, while serving with 111 (AC) Squadron at RCAF Station, Patricia Bay, BC, during 1940. No.428 carried out the squadron's first operation of the war on 29 June 1940 when it reported sighting a submarine off Otter Point. The Lysander remained on RCAF strength until December 1946. (Via David H. Smith)

A general view of the snow-covered apron at Rockcliffe shows at least a dozen Lysanders belonging to 112 and 123 Squadrons. (Via David H. Smith)

Into RCAF service

The first Canadian-built Lysander Mk II was No.416, which was delivered to the RCAF on 7 September 1939, just three days before Canada declared war on Germany. On that day, the order was raised to 75 Lysander Mk IIs, which would be serialled 416 to 490. Early flight trials went according to plan for the Lysander – other than the fact that it was not up to the job of coping with a Canadian winter! The cockpit was redesigned with an improved heating system, and the original draughty canopy was upgraded to make life considerably more comfortable for the crew.

110 (Army Co-operation) Squadron, RCAF, was the first recipient of the Canadian Lysander Mk II and was also the first unit to be ordered into service overseas. The squadron sailed from Halifax, Nova Scotia, on 16 February, leaving its aircraft behind, bound for Liverpool, which was reached ten days later. On 27 February, 110 Squadron arrived at Old Sarum by train, where it was issued with 12 Lysander Mk IIs, which were taken from RAF stock. Despite 'high jinks' by the Canadians, accidents where rare, and the unit's first loss was the result of mechanical failure rather than fooling around. On 19 March 1940, the Perseus engine of Mk II N1316 failed after taking off from Old Sarum, and a forced landing was successfully made near Salisbury, resulting in a collapsed undercarriage but no injuries to the two crew.

After an exuberant period during the 'Phoney War', the Canadians began to receive news of how their RAF colleagues had faired during the Battle of France; it was not encouraging. In the meantime, at Malton, 12 Canadian Lysander Mk IIs were being dismantled and crated to compensate for the dozen taken from RAF stocks. In the end, only six (Nos. 434 and 436 to 440) actually managed to cross the Atlantic, and on arrival they were taken on RAF strength as DG442 to DG447, but all briefly served with 112 Squadron RCAF.

Ex-RAF Lysander Mk II, R9003, in service with 110 Squadron RCAF at Odiham. The aircraft was returned to the RAF, converted into a target tug and went on to serve with 2 AOS and 7 AGS. (Via David H. Smith)

Trials unit

On 9 June 1940, 110 Squadron was moved to Odiham, where, at first, the unit was used by the RAF as a specialist Lysander trials unit. One example of this new role was when the prototype K6127 was attached to the unit while it carried a pair of 20mm Oerlikon cannons from 13 July. During the same period, 110 Squadron was also employed to carry out anti-invasion patrols, which was a common task for UK-based Lysander squadrons at that time. Operational training also continued including dive-bombing practice, which brought about the demise of Lysander Mk II, N1301 on 17 July 1940. The pilot of N1301 pulled out of his dive too late, struck some trees and crashed at Forest Row in Sussex. 110 Squadron also became the first operational unit to receive the Lysander Mk III when R9001 to R9009 were delivered on 23 August. Out of this batch, which was a partial replacement for their original Lysander Mk IIs, only one aircraft was lost. On 23 January 1941, Mk III, R9004, lost height after a night take-off, crashed and burst into flames two miles west of Odiham. All of the remainder went on to further service with multiple units, and five were later converted into target tugs. Further Mk III Lysanders were delivered during 1940, but by April 1941, 110 Squadron was re-equipped with the Curtiss Tomahawk, although at least four Lysanders remained on strength at the time.

One of 57 ex-RAF Lysander Mk III TTs transferred to the RCAF in 1942 and re-serialled 1536–1592. Although yet to be confirmed, 1589 could be ex-V9281, which originally served 1 SAC and 41 OTU as a Mk IIIA. (Via David H. Smith)

The Canadian Prime Minister, the Right Honourable William Lyon Mackenzie King (centre in fur coat), inspects the aircraft of 110 Squadron RCAF at Rockcliffe. The aircraft behind is the second production Lysander Mk II, 417. (Via David H. Smith)

Canadian Lysander expansion

While 110 Squadron worked up at Rockcliffe, a second unit, 111 (Thunderbird) Squadron, was mobilised on 10 September 1939 and moved to Patricia Bay with a few Atlas aircraft on strength. These were joined by four Lysanders, which remained with the unit until January 1941. 118 Squadron followed when it first received Lysanders at Saint John from December 1939. The few Lysanders on strength had gone by August 1940, when 118 Squadron was supposed to be redesignated as a fighter squadron, but this never came to fruition and the unit was disbanded in late September 1940.

Next to receive the Lysander was 112 (City of Winnipeg) Squadron which, like 118 Squadron, was mobilided on 10 September 1939 and moved to Rockcliffe, where it was attached to the Canadian Active Service Force in readiness for service overseas. The first Lysanders were delivered to 112 Squadron in March 1940, and by the time the unit reached Britain, France had already fallen and the unit was relegated to training duties until the end of the year. By then, the unit was redesignated as 2 (Fighter) Squadron at Digby and ultimately became 402 (Fighter) Squadron.

1941 saw two brand-new RCAF squadrons formed, both with Lysanders. The first was 400 (City of Toronto) Squadron at Odiham on 1 March 1941 with the Lysander Mk III. The unit was actually 110 Squadron RCAF renumbered; the first of 70 new squadrons – generally all from a Commonwealth background – that were integrated into the RAF for the remainder of World War Two. 400 Squadron operated the Lysander Mk III until December 1941, alongside the Tomahawk Mk I, IIA and IIB, which remained on strength until July 1942, by which time the Mustang Mk I continued the unit's original army co-operation role.

The second unit to be formed in 1941 was created from scratch at Croydon on 12 August 1941. 414 (Sarnia Imperials) was initially equipped with the Lysander Mk III and the Tomahawk Mk I and Mk II. Both were ultimately replaced by the highly capable Mustang Mk I in June 1942.

The remainder of the RCAF's Lysander units were all formed in January 1942 and would remain at home in Canada. These were 121, 122 and 123 squadrons, the last operating as the School of Army Co-operation from Rockcliffe. Both 121 and 122 Squadron operated the Lysander Mk II TT until March 1944, while the Lysander was gone from the strength of 123 Squadron by June 1943.

Thanks to the amount of Lysanders built in Canada during World War Two and the nature of their duties, there were more examples extant in that country than anywhere else in the world. The very last RCAF Lysander was not SOC until 13 December 1946. Several were released onto the civilian market during the late 1940s, and at least half a dozen became crop sprayers.

Originally constructed as a Lysander Mk IIIA by Victory Aircraft, No.2322 was one of a batch of 150 aircraft built from late 1941 through to September 1942. Many of the Victory-built 'Lizzies' were converted to TT standard, complete with the effective very high-visibility black and yellow livery. (Via David H. Smith)

Left: It is not clear whether it was adapted in any great quantity, but at least one RCAF Lysander was trialled with skis instead of its conventional wheeled undercarriage. The aircraft in question was Lysander Mk II, 459, and like the Finnish Air Force machines, there is no reason why the skis would not have been successful. (Via David H. Smith)

Below: An RCAF armourer unloads the port .303in Browning machine gun of a Lysander Mk II at Rockcliffe. (Via David H. Smith)

An RCAF air gunner demonstrates his Fairey-mounted 0.303in (7.7mm) Lewis machine gun, which was the standard rear defensive armament of the Lysander Mk II. Note that, even from this angle, the air gunner's field of fire is poor, and he was powerless to stop an attack from low and below. Therefore, other than making incredibly tight turns, the Lysander's real hope for survival was down low. (Via Martyn Chorlton)

A busy scene as an RCAF Lysander is subjected to major maintenance, which would have been conducted more frequently due to the harsh environment in Canada. Healthy production and a training role without any risk of enemy action resulted in more Lysanders being extant in Canada during the post-war period than any other country in the world. (Via Martyn Chorlton)

RCAF UNITS

110 (City of Toronto) Sqn

A/c: Mk II, December 1939 to August 1940; Mk III, August 1940 to February 1941

Codes: AY and SP

Bases: Rockcliffe (Ottawa), Old Sarum, Odiham and Redhill

A/c: (Mk II), L4788–L4790; N1209; N1220; N1265; N1267; N1268 and N1301 (Lost 17 July 1940); RCAF serials 417; 428; 429; 432 and 433; N1316 (Lost 19 March 1940); P1694–P1698; P1730–P1732; P1743; P9095; P9104; (Mk III), P9113; P9114; P9116; P9123; P9125; P9128; R9001–R9009 (R9004 lost 23 January 1941); R9116; R9117; R9119; R9120; T1434; T1443; T1448; T1460; T1563 and T1564

111 (Thunderbird) Sqn

A/c: Mk II, December 1939 to January 1941

Code: TM

Base: Patricia Bay (Vancouver)

A/c: (Mk II), 434–440 and P1729

112 (City of Winnipeg) Sqn

A/c: Mk II, March 1940 to December 1940

Code: XO and AE

Base: Rockcliffe

A/c: (Mk II 'XO'), 416; 420 and 436–44; (Mk II 'AE'), 436–440; P1729; P9178

118 Sqn

A/c: Mk II, December 1939 to August 1940

Base: Saint John

A/c: (Mk II), 422; 423 and 430–432

121 Sqn*

A/c: Mk II TT, January 1942 to March 1944

Code: EN

Base: Dartmouth

A/c: (Mk II TT), 418; 450; 1559 and V9519

*When re-formed, 121 Squadron was created from the Eastern Air Command Communications Flight and the Target Towing Flight. By July and August 1942, respectively, the unit also comprised a Rescue and Salvage Flight and a Calibration Flight.

122 Sqn**

A/c: Mk II TT, January 1942 to March 1944

Code: AG

Base: Patricia Bay

A/c: (Mk II TT), 416; 446; 483 and 485

**Formed as a composite unit from Western Air Command Coast Artillery Co-operation and Communications Flight.

123 (Army Co-operation) Sqn***
A/c: Mk II, January 1942 to June 1943
Code: VD
Base: Rockcliffe
A/c: (Mk II), 421; 454; 477 and 488
***Formed as the School of Army Co-operation; redesignated 123 (Army Co-operation Training) Squadron on 15 January 1942.

400 (City of Toronto) Sqn, *Percussuri Vigiles (On the watch to strike)*
A/c: Mk III, March 1941 to April 1941
Bases: Odiham, Redhill, Gatwick, Bottisham and Weston Zoyland
A/c: (Mk III), R9001; R9002; R9005–R9007; R9009; R9119; P9125; T1434; T1436 (Lost 10 May 1941); (Mk IIIA), V9373

414 (Sarnia Imperials) Sqn, *Totis Virbis (Will all our might)*
A/c: Mk III, August 1941 to June 1942
Base: Croydon
A/c: (Mk III), R9112; T1563; T1671; (Mk IIIA), V9381; V9382; V9445; V9516 and V9586

32 OTU
A/c: Mk II, August 1941 to 1944; Mk IIIA, August 1941 to 1944
Base: Patricia Bay

RCAF Bombing and Gunnery Schools operating Lysanders
No.1, Jarvis, Ontario; No.2, Mossbank, Saskatchewan; No.3 MacDonald, Manitoba; No.4 Fingal, Ontario; No.5 Dafoe, Saskatchewan; No.6, Mountain View, Ontario; No.7 Paulson, Manitoba; No.8 Lethbridge, Alberta; No.9 Mont Joli, Quebec and No.31 Picton, Quebec.

Lysanders in RCAF service from 1939 to 1946

Serial	Number	Mark	Notes
416–490	75	II	Constructed by the NSCC
	700	II	Pattern aircraft; ex-R2047
1536–1592	*57	III TT	Ex-RAF machines transferred to RCAF from 1942
2305–2454	150	IIIA	Constructed by Victory Aircraft

*These ex-RAF aircraft were: P1728 (1578); V9281; V9285; V9290; V9294; V9298; V9300; V9301; V9306; V9307; V9312–V9315; V9317; V9318; V9320; V9323; V9324; V9327; V9329; V9351; V9352; V9354; V9355; V9357; V9358; V9365; V9366; V9368; V9370; V9371; V9374; V9378; V9383; V9386; V9404; V9407; V9409; V9412; V9413; V9415; V9416-V9419; V9422; V9423; V9425; V9432; V9442; V9443; V9446; V9449; V9476; V9477; V9480; V9481; V9486; V9501; V9502; V9504; V9508; V9509; V9518–V9521; V9539; V9546; V9552–V9554; V9556; V9570; V9577; V9582; V9589; V9607; V9613; V9642; V9643; V9645; V9647; V9651–V9653; V9676; V9678; V9712; V9713; V9716; V9719; V9730–V9734; V9739; V9746; V9747 and V9750

Chapter 11

African Skies

Moderate expansion

During the RAF's major expansion programme in 1936, the Air Ministry proposed that no more than 24 Westland Lysanders would be needed to cover the Middle Eastern region. The only army co-operation unit in the area at the time was 208 Squadron, which was flying the Hawker Audax

Lysander Mk I L4729 was one of the original batch of 24 aircraft that were taken straight from the Yeovil production line and shipped direct to Heliopolis in November 1938. After service with 208 Squadron, the Lysander worked for 205 Group until 21 February 1942, when the engine failed after take-off, forcing the aircraft to ditch off Dekheila. (Via author)

and had operated from Heliopolis since 1934. Twelve of the brand-new Lysanders would be used to replace the Audax, while the remainder would be held at an RAF depot at Heliopolis as a war reserve. The aircraft, Lysander Mk Is, were serialled L4707 to L4730, and as they left the Yeovil production line they were placed straight into packing cases and shipped to Egypt, arriving in November 1938.

It was not 208 Squadron that flew the type first but a pair of pilots from 6 Squadron, a unit that was equipped with the Hawker Hardy at Ramleh in the British Mandate of Palestine. Trouble was brewing between the Arabs and the Jews in Palestine, and 6 Squadron were called upon to evaluate if the Lysander would be suitable for the anti-terrorist role. The two unidentified aircraft were tested by several 6 Squadron pilots over Christmas 1938, all of them returning favourable reports.

208 Squadron undertook conversion training from the Audax to the Lysander from December through to January 1939. Fully converted, the unit continued 'working up' into the spring of 1939, suffering its first Lysander loss on 31 March when Mk I L4718 stalled during a message pick-up exercise and crashed, luckily without injury to the crew.

Increasing Lysander strength as war breaks

By mid-1939, it was obvious another world war was inevitable, and despite the fact that the conflict would germinate in Europe the Air Ministry wisely decided to increase the number of Lysanders in the Middle East to 48 aircraft. This number was designed to cover the Lysanders already in service with 208 Squadron and the handful with 6 Squadron, which would take the type on in larger numbers from September 1939, alongside their original Hardys and several Gloster Gauntlet Mk I and Mk II fighters. Lysander Mk Is were already becoming plentiful at home, as units such as 16 Squadron re-equipped with the Mk II, and as a result a large number of 'second-hand' Mk Is were transferred to the Middle East.

When the war began, 208 Squadron was expecting to be recalled to the European Theatre, but the Commander-in-Chief, RAF Middle East, Air Marshal Sir William Mitchell stepped in to stop it from happening. Having already trained intensely with the 7th Armoured Division (the 'Desert Rats'), Mitchell correctly argued that 208 Squadron should remain with the unit they had already exercised with in an environment where the usefulness of army co-operation was fully appreciated. 6 Squadron were also of the same mindset, thinking that they would be returned to operate in Europe, but like 208 Squadron they were destined to remain in theatre for the entire war and beyond.

Allies flex their muscles

The war began quietly for the Allies throughout North Africa and the Middle East, with forces concentrating on conducting exercises in preparation for the inevitable contact with the enemy, which by May 1940 was still only the Germans. Between 7 and 17 May 1940, a very large-scale Nile Delta Defence Exercise was performed in Egypt. On 22 May, one of the RAF's largest 'show of strength' exercises took place when a formation of 72 Blenheims, 63 Gladiators, ten Sunderlands and 21 Lysanders flew over Giza, Cairo, and the Abdin Palace before breaking up over Heliopolis. This flypast was clearly an indication that the RAF in the region was ready for action, and suspicions were already in place that the Italians could enter the war on the side of the Germans depending on how quickly the latter would sweep through Europe. Mussolini saw his chance when France fell, and, on 10 June 1940, Italy finally showed its hand and declared war on Britain. This was two years earlier than Mussolini had originally planned, and while the British were more than ready to begin moving their forces west, the Italians were far from ready to begin an assault to the east.

202 Group into action

The commander of 202 Group, Air Cdre Raymond Collishaw, did not waste any time and rather than waiting for the Italians, he ordered an attack on enemy airfields using Blenheims from 45, 55, 113 and 211 squadrons escorted by the Gladiators of 80 and 112 squadrons. Collishaw's remaining assets in the region were the Bombay transports of 216 Squadron and 208 Squadron's Lysanders. Well-versed in desert operations, 208 Squadron was a mobile force, and its war role saw the ground elements of the unit divided into a pair of echelons. The first comprised over 30 Ford two- and three-ton trucks loaded with enough supplies to support the entire squadron for seven days. The second echelon was made up of six-wheel Fordson and Crossley trucks loaded with tents and maintenance equipment, which could also serve as a supply column should the squadron need to operate longer from its home base.

208 Squadron began operations by reporting on enemy positions, but this type of sortie would need a fighter escort if the Lysander was to have any longevity in the region. These sorties were often expensive as losses were incurred by Lysanders and their escorting fighters, such as on 22 June, when a Gladiator was shot down by a Fiat CR.42. But every now and then, a Lysander would become the attacker; one example being on 28 July when a single aircraft was looking for a missing 11th Hussars patrol. En-route, the Lysander crew spotted an Italian aircraft landing in the desert to assist another which had force-landed east of El Adem. Swooping down, the pilot of the Lysander strafed with his front guns and then banked to give his gunner a chance to hit both of the Italian machines. As the Italians scattered into the desert, the persistent Lysander crew managed to set both enemy aircraft alight before returning to their original task.

Several ferocious dogfights took place between escorting Gladiators and attacking CR.42s during August 1940, and while the biplane fighters were suffering losses the Lysander generally managed to make their escape. Only one 208 Squadron Lysander was lost during the month, when Mk I L4685 suffered an engine failure on 29 August.

Operations stepped up a gear when the Italian ground forces began to push out from Libya on 13 September, and additional aircraft had bolstered their air force. While only one Lysander, Mk I L4711, was damaged by flak and damaged beyond repair after force-landing during the entire month, October 1940 saw 208 Squadron's attrition rate begin to increase. On 15 October, two aircraft, Lysander Mk Is L4714 and L4717, were brought down by CR.42s, the former near Giarabub and the latter on the Libyan border. One of these two aircraft suffered 208 Squadron's first fatal casualties when Plt Off D. M. B. Druce and Sgt J. F. Muldowney were killed. On 16 October, a third Lysander Mk I, L4686, was shot down by CR.42s near Maktila. This intensive period of activity continued into November 1940, beginning with the loss of another Lysander at Siwa following a bombing raid by 18 SM.79s, which destroyed one aircraft, L4721, and damaged several others.

Bolstering army co-operation

208 Squadron's workload began to ease through November 1940, aided by the unit's 'C' Flight being re-equipped with the Hawker Hurricane for tactical reconnaissance work, although the Lysander would remain with the unit until May 1942. 3 Squadron, RAAF, also arrived in theatre with one of its flights equipped with Lysanders, and 6 Squadron, still located in Palestine, was preparing to move to the Western Desert. 6 Squadron had 13 Lysanders, two Gauntlets and a single Hardy on strength when 'C' Flight was ordered to move to Qasaba in Egypt for operational training. 'A' and 'B' Flights of 6 Squadron remained in Palestine, where they were busily employed flying coastal anti-submarine patrols and army co-operation duties with the Arab Legion.

6 Squadron operated the Lysander on two separate occasions, first from September 1939 to June 1941 and then from August 1941 to January 1942. It was during the latter period that Mk II P9073 saw service until it was lost in action on 13 December 1941. (Via author)

6 Squadron's 'C' Flight joined the fray from early October 1940 through to December when 'B' Flight took over. Not long after, 6 Squadron suffered its first casualties when Lysander Mk II, L6877 went missing during a reconnaissance sortie to Fort Maddalena; Flt Lt D. T. St. H. Davies and Sgt R. Chantry were believed to have been buried next to the wreck of their aircraft.

Another unnecessary loss was caused by a lack of supply dropping equipment on 9 February 1941, when 6 Squadron's Lysander Mk II, P9188 was called up to look for a missing tank after a skirmish near Mersa Matruh. Forced to land near the tank, the Lysander hit a cairn on landing, which wrecked the undercarriage.

Supporting Greece

During February 1941, the number of Lysanders in theatre reduced when 208 Squadron was withdrawn to Greece when Italian forces invaded from neighbouring Albania. 208 Squadron's tasking was transferred to 'A' and 'B' Flights of 6 Squadron, which was now operating from Tobruk under direct control of HQ, 202 Group. The squadron's own HQ and 'C' Flight were also moved from Palestine to Heliopolis.

During March 1941, 'A' Flight of 6 Squadron began to receive the Hurricane at Agedabia, while 'B' Flight retained its Lysanders at Barce, which had been home since 24 February. The arrival of Gen Erwin Rommel in North Africa temporarily changed the dynamic, and a tactical withdrawal of British and Commonwealth troops was ordered until forces were built up again. Lysanders played an important role, as Tobruk quickly became besieged by the enemy during April and May 1941. As well

as artillery-spotting, the Lysanders still continued to fly long-range tactical reconnaissance sorties, including one on 9 April whilst operating from El Gubbi West. During this particular sortie, flown by Plt Off J. E. McFall with Cpl Copley as air gunner, a Junkers Ju 52 was shot down.

Final fling from Tobruk

The main German and Italian ground assault on Tobruk came on 11 April, followed by waves of enemy aircraft from 14 April onwards, which were greeted by a depleting number of 73 Squadron Hurricanes. Barce came under regular attack by the Luftwaffe during this period, and on 22 April, Mk IIs L6875

267 Squadron was re-formed at Heliopolis on 20 August 1940 from the Heliopolis Communications Flight. The squadron flew an incredible range of aircraft, which even included enemy machines and of course the Lysander Mk I and Mk II. This is Mk II P9191, which only served with 267 Squadron, at El Kabrit on 10 February 1943. The Lysander served the squadron until June 1945. (Via author)

and L6876 were both destroyed when the airfield was evacuated. From 25 April, the remaining four serviceable Hurricanes of 73 Squadron were flown out of Tobruk, leaving just 6 Squadron with a handful of Lysanders, Hurricanes and a single Magister.

Regular air attacks made operations impossible, and on 19 May the remaining four 6 Squadron Lysanders were withdrawn along with Magister. The small formation was fired on by its own anti-aircraft guns as they crossed Tobruk harbour, but all reached Maaten Bagush safely.

From June 1941, 6 Squadron became an all-Hurricane unit, and the operational days of the Lysander came to an end.

Chapter 12

The Lysander's Final Victory

The Royal Egyptian Air Force

Established in 1939, the REAF, having broken away from army control, began its modernisation programme by ordering 18 brand-new Lysander Mk Is, serials Y500 to Y517, and one ex-RAF machine, R2650, which was re-serialled Y518. A 20th and final Lysander, ex-RAF Mk III, R9000, was also acquired by the REAF but does not appear to have gained a local serial.

The new Lysanders entered service with 1 (General Purpose) Squadron at Almaza on the edge of Cairo, which was also occupied by the RAF's 208 Squadron. After conversion training, aided by the

RAF, 1 Squadron was redesignated as an army co-operation unit. By the end of January 1939, the unit was declared operational under the command of Sqn Ldr Salih Mahmud Salih, a position he would hold throughout the majority of World War Two.

Controlled by British forces at the outbreak of the war, 1 Squadron carried out its army co-operation duties effectively throughout the region, and all 18 Lysanders remained serviceable until conditions began to take their toll by late 1940. As serviceability began to suffer, it was probably around this period that the two additional ex-RAF machines were allocated to the REAF to keep the small force going. By late 1942, the REAF Lysanders were down to 14, which, incredibly, continued in service until 1945, although they were only good for target-towing and searchlight co-operation duties. By 1944, 1 Squadron had begun to re-equip with ex-RAF Hurricanes, while the last Lysanders on strength took part in convoy protection exercises, and two were retained as hacks into 1945.

The shiny new Lysander Mk Is of 1 (Army Co-operation) Squadron, Royal Egyptian Air Force (REAF), on parade for inspection by the director of the air force, Brig Ali Islam Bey. The British described Bey as 'pleasant but totally ineffective', while 1 Squadron's commander, Sqn Ldr Salih Mahmud Salih, was applauded as an 'outstanding officer'. (Via David H. Smith)

The Arab-Israeli War

While the war in Europe had finally come to end, peace was destined only to rein for a short period, as relations with Britain began to deteriorate and disputes over the frontier of Palestine also increased. For good reason, the REAF kept hold of as many aircraft as possible, and by early 1946 13 Lysanders were still recorded on strength. Nine of them were deemed beyond economic repair and were scrapped between October 1946 and January 1947, while the remaining four were selected for overhaul and brought back up to an airworthy condition. All four were later attached to the REAF Royal Flight, which became the nucleus for 3 (Communications) Squadron. In the meantime, the original Lysander unit, 1 Squadron, was re-equipped with the Spitfire LF.IX from early 1947.

As trouble began to build in the region, the REAF realised that it had a very limited photographic-reconnaissance capability, and it was decided that two of the surviving Lysanders would be converted to this role in early 1948. Keeping these two machines serviceable seems to have been quite a challenge, but this was not the only problem for the REAF. Only a handful, if any, REAF officers were actually trained as photographic interpreters, and no mention is given about processing and printing support.

The first phase of the Arab-Israeli War began on 15 May 1948; the previous day, following the termination of the British Mandate of Palestine, David Ben-Gurion had declared a new Jewish State to be known as the State of Israel. The initial phase was over by 11 June, resulting in a truce (the first), which would last until 8 July; whether the REAF's small Lysander force flew any sorties is not known, but one had an amazing encounter with a 101 Squadron, Israeli Air Force Avia S-199 (aka C.210; effectively a Messerschmitt Bf 109G powered by a Junkers Jumo engine) on 9 July 1948.

Only 20 Lysanders entered service with the REAF, the first arriving in 1939. Numbers had reduced to 14 by 1942 but were maintained at that level until 1945. The post-war survivors were reduced by another nine, while four were refurbished and pressed back into service by 1947/48. (Via David H. Smith)

Enemy encounter

A single Lysander, flown by one of the first three pilots to serve with the REAF, Air Cdre Muhammad Abd al-Munaim Miqaati, was detailed to fly from al-Arish to Cairo-Almaza. The war, which was now in its second phase, was destined to be over by 18 July and is traditionally known as the Ten-Day War. Miqaati takes up the story of that day's remarkable sortie:

It was Condition Red. I had been advised to keep the radio on, but I was still nervous as I set across the Mediterranean. Fortunately my gunner – I don't remember his name – was a keen-sighted man and he spotted an Israeli Messerschmitt as it manoeuvred into position to attack. Of course, my Lysander was a very old kind of airplane, but I'd flown these for a long time. Still, we were at a big disadvantage and you'd expect such a contest could only end one way… The pilot of the Israeli aircraft came up behind us. I told my gunner to fire just as the Messerschmitt came into range and I went down to about 100ft. Then the gunner fired and I throttled right back. You know the Lysander can drop like a stone to land in a field, like they did when the RAF took spies in and out of France. The Israeli must have been concentrating on keeping me in his sights because he dropped his nose to follow. He overshot and went right in, almost level with me. I honestly felt sick in my stomach and, I don't know why, I saluted him. Then we flew straight back to Cairo.

For the Israelis, the loss of one of its aircraft and its pilot that day was a mystery. The loss of the pilot, Bob Vickman, an American born in Hollywood, California, was a huge blow to the fledgling 101 Squadron, which had only been formed with its Czech-Built S-199s in May 1948. Not long after Vickman's loss, it was discovered that the twin upper fuselage machine guns of the unit's S-199s had not been properly synchronised, and as a result when they were fired the propeller would either be badly holed or even shot away. One theory to explain the American pilots plunge into the sea was that he accidentally shot away his own propeller, as the gunner of the Lysander never made any claim to actually shooting down the fighter. However, not taking anything away from Miqaati's flying skills, the incredible low speed that a 'Lizzie' could achieve would not have been something Vickman would have come across before.

This incident was possibly one of the last flings for the Lysander in combat, and, by October 1948, 3 Squadron had no Lysanders remaining on strength and only a single aircraft was recorded as being serviceable at Almaza in January 1950. It is possible that this unidentified Lysander was one of several historic aircraft planned for a new air museum that never came to fruition because of the Egyptian Revolution of 1952. Unfortunately, most of the REAF's early aviation was destroyed by the RAF during the Suez campaign in 1956, making this particular Lysander also the last to be destroyed by 'enemy' action.

Bob Vickman joined the USAAF in 1943 and served with a photographic-reconnaissance unit in the Pacific Theatre until the end of World War Two. Vickman was one of many Jewish Americans who volunteered to join the new Israeli Air Force, and after training in Czechoslovakia he joined 101 Squadron in early June 1948. His death remained a mystery to the Israelis until Air Cdre Muhammad Abd al-Munaim Miqaati's account was published many years later. (Via David H. Smith)

Appendix 1

The Westland Lysander Production Summary

Westland P.8 Lysander prototypes (Specification A.39/34): Two prototypes, K6127 (first flown 15 June 1936) and K6728 (first flown 11 October 1936). K6127, after being brought up to production standard, was experimentally fitted with two 20mm Oerlikon guns on the undercarriage in 1940, and later modified with tail (dummy) turret and Delanne tandem wing. K6128 went to Middle East and India for tropical trials, 1938–39.

Westland Lysander Mk I (Specification A.36/36): 169 aircraft with 890hp Bristol Mercury XII engines. L4673–L4738, P1665–P1699, R2572, R2575–R2600 and R2612–R2652. R2650 to Royal Egyptian Air Force. Converted to TT Mk Is: R2572, R2575, R2578, R2S81, R2587, R2588, R2589, R2591, R2593, R2594, R2597, R2598, R2632 and R2638. Converted to TT Mk IIIs: P1666, P1668, P1680, P1681, P1683, R2651 and R2652.

Westland Lysander Mk II: 442 aircraft with 905hp Bristol Perseus XII engines. L4739–L4816, L6847–L6888, N1200–N1227, N1240–N1276, N1289–N1320, P1711–P1745, P90S1–P9080, P9095–P9140, P9176–P9199, R1987–R2010, R2025–R2047: also 3101–3136 of the Turkish Air Force, 61–66 of the Irish Air Corps, and '01' of the Armee de l'Air. L4798, L6869, N1208, N1248, N1300, P1713, P1735, P1736, P1738, P9059, P9078, P9102, P9103, P9134, P9181, P9184, R2036, R2039, R2040, R2043, R2045 and R2046 transferred to the Free French Forces. P9105 fitted with Blackburn–Steiger high-lift wing. Modified to TT Mk IIs: L6867, N1289, N1320, P9099 and R1998. Converted to TT Mk IIIs: N1289, N1320, P1715, P9109, P9110, P9111, P9113, P9114, P9115, P9117, P9123, P9125, P9126, P9128, P9130 and P9133. R2047 as pattern aircraft to Canada, January 1940.

Westland Lysander Mk II (Canadian licence-built): 75 aircraft with 905hp Bristol Perseus XII engines. 416–490 (438–440 became DG44J–DG447). Westland Lysander Mk III. 100 aircraft with 870hp Bristol Mercury XX engines. R8991–R9030, R9056–R9079, R9100–R9135. R8991–R8999 to Finland; R9000 to Egypt.

Westland Lysander Mk III: 250 aircraft with 870hp Bristol Mercury XX engines. T1422–T1470, T1501–T1535, T1548–T1590, T1610–T1655, T1670–71709, T1735–T1771. Converted to TT Mk IIIs: T1445, T1450, T1453, T1456, T1458, T1461, T1532, T1534, T1571, T1583, T1616, T1623, T1626, T1633, T1642, T1674–T1679, T1688, T1692, T1699, T1746, T1750, T1752 and T1763. To Admiralty charge: T1570 as TT Mk III; T1739 used for British Overseas Airways Corporation crew training.

Westland Lysander Mk III: 17 aircraft built by Westland (Doncaster) Ltd. W6939–W6945, W6951–W6960. A further 483 aircraft between W6675 and VV6938, and between W6961 and W7241 were cancelled. Westland Lysander Mk III (Canadian licence-built). 150 aircraft with 870hp Bristol Mercury 30 engines. 2305–2454.

Westland Lysander Mk IIIA: 347 aircraft with 870hp Bristol Mercury 30 engines. V9280–V9329, V9347–V9386, V9401–V9450, V9472–V9521, V9538–V9557, V9570–V9619, V9642–V9681, V9704–V9750. V9506, V9583 and V9741 to United States Army Air Forces. V9614 supplied to Free French Forces. V9372, V9579, V9679 and V9726 converted to tow gliders. Supplied to Portugal: V9309, V9321, V9363, V9439, V9555, V9594, V9705 and V9729.

Westland Lysander TT Mk IIIA: 100 aircraft with 870hp Bristol Mercury 30 engines. V9751–V9753, V9775–V9824, V9844–V9868 and V9885–V9906.

Total Lysander production: Two prototypes plus 1,650 production aircraft (1,366 delivered to the RAF).

'Briefing a Lysander Crew'. The pilots are just off on a reconnaissance. The AILO explains the purpose of the flight, the area to be reconnoitered, and what is to be looked for. (Via Martyn Chorlton)

Home and Away: Lysander Units

Lysander service with the RAF, FAA and Foreign Air Forces* from 1938 to 1947.

Royal Air Force

2 Sqn, *Hereward*
A/c: Mk I, July 1938 to February 1940; Mk II, February 1940 to September 1940; Mk III, September 1940 to July 1942
Codes: KO and XV
Bases: Hawkinge, Abbeville/Drucat, Senon, Ronchin, Lubuissière, Wevelghem, Boulogne, Lympne, Bekesbourne, Hatfield, Cambridge, Sawbridgeworth, Firbeck, Weston Zoyland, Martlesham Heath, and Gatwick

4 Sqn, *In future videre (To see into the future)*
A/c: Mk II, December 1938 to September 1940; Mk III, September 1940 to July 1941; Mk IIIA, May 1941 to June 1942
Codes: TV and FY
Bases: Odiham, Mons-en-Chaussée, Ronchin, Aspelaere, Clairmarais, Dunkirk, Detling, Ringway, Linton-on-Ouse and Clifton

---

* RCAF, IAF and REAF service covered in separate chapters

6 Sqn, *Oculi exercitus (The eyes of the Army)*
A/c: Mk I, September 1939 to December 39; Mk II, February 1940 to June 1941
Code: JV
Bases: Ramleh, Qasaba, Siwa, Tobruk, Aqir, Heliopolis, Agedabia, Antelat, Msus, Marawa, Derna, El Gubbi East, El Gubbi West and Maaten Bagush

13 Sqn, *Adjuvamus tuendo (We assist by watching)*
A/c: Mk II, January 1939 to January 1941; Mk III, November 1940 to July 1941
Codes: AN and OO
Bases: Odiham, Mons-en-Chaussée, Flamicourt, Douai, Abbeville, Clairmarais, Châteaubriant, Bekesbourne, Hooton Park and Speke

16 Sqn, *Operta Aperta (Hidden things are revealed)*
A/c: Mk I, May 1938 to April 1939 and May 1940 to September 1940; Mk II, April 1939 to November 1940; Mk III, October 1940 to July 1941; Mk IIIA, May 1941 to July 1942
Codes: KJ, EE and UG
Bases: Old Sarum, Hawkinge, Amiens, Bertangles, Lympne, Redhill, Cambridge, Okehampton, Weston Zoyland, Roborough Tilshead, St Just, Bolt Head, Lee-on-Solent, Thruxton and Farnborough

20 Sqn, *Facta non verba (Deeds not words)*
A/c: Mk II, December 1941 to April 1943
Code: HN
Bases: Begumpet, Peshawar, Chakulia, Jamshedpur, Tezpur, Dinjan, Feni, Imphal, Chittagong, Charra and Maungdaw

T1631 'XV-H' was a Lysander Mk III that was delivered new to 2 Squadron in late 1940. Later converted to a target tug the aircraft served with 289 Squadron and 7 AGS; the latter until September 1940. (Via Martyn Chorlton)

'B' Flight of 26 Squadron at rest at Ronaldsway during the summer of 1939, during a brief detachment from Catterick. (Via Martyn Chorlton)

26 Sqn, *N wagter in die Lug (A guard in the sky)*
A/c: Mk II, February 1939 to November 1940; Mk III, November 1940 to June 1942
Codes: HL and RM
Bases: Catterick, Ronaldsway, Abbeville/Drucat, Ronchin, Dieppe, Arras, Laon/Athies, Lympne, West Malling, Cambridge, Odiham, Gatwick, Weston Zoyland, Leconfield, Detling, Warmwell, Barton Bendish, Twinwood Farm, Upwood, Snailwell, Honington, Manston and Madley

28 Sqn, *Quicquid agas age (Whatsoever you may do, do)*
A/c: Mk II, September 1941 to December 1942
Code: BF
Bases: Kohat, Lashio, Zayatkwin, Port Blair, Magwe, Mingaladon, Asansol, Lahore, Ranchi, Dum Dum and Jamshedpur

116 Sqn, *Precision in Defence*
A/c: Mk II, February 1941 to March 1943
Code: II
Bases: Hatfield, Hendon, Heston and Croydon

138 Sqn, *For freedom*
A/c: Mk IIIA, August 1941 to March 1942
Code: NF
Bases: Newmarket and Stradishall

148 Sqn, *Trusty*
A/c: Mk IIIA, February 1944 to May 1945
Code: FS
Bases: Brindisi and Calvi

161 Sqn, *Liberate*
A/c: Mk IIIA, February 1942 to June 1945
Code: MA
Bases: Newmarket, Graveley, Tempsford and Tangmere

173 Sqn, *Quocumque (Whithersoever)*
A/c: Mk II, July 1942 to July 1943
Base: Heliopolis

208 Sqn, *Vigilant*
A/c: Mk I, January 1939 to May 1942; Mk II, January 1939 to May 1942
Bases: Heliopolis, Mersah Matruh, Qasaba, Sidi Barrani, Bir Kanayis, Siwa, Halfaya, Bir Mella, Gambut, Tmimi, Mechili, Agedabia, Marawa, Barce, Kazaklar, Larissa, Pharsala, Amphiklia, Kalamaki, Argos, Maleme, Aboukir, Gaza, Habbaniyah, Amman, H.4, Haifa, Ramleh, Muqueibila, Rosh Pinna, Rayak, Deir-es-Zor, Aqir, LG 10, Gabr Saleh, LG 75, LG 112, LG 134, LG 123, LG 128, El Gubbi, LG 131, Antelat, Msus, Benina, Martuba, Acroma, Sidi Azeiz, Bir el Regal, El Adem and Moascar

225 Sqn, *We guide the sword*
A/c: Mk II, October 1939 to September 1940; Mk III, September 1940 to June 1942
Codes: LX and WU
Bases: Odiham, Old Sarum, Tilshead, Okehampton, Shoreham, Pembrey, Exeter, Staverton, Thruxton, Weston Zoyland, Dumfries and Abbotsinch

231 Sqn, *Prepared to Attack*
A/c: Mk II, July 1940 to August 1941; Mk III, November 1940 to May 1943
Code: VM
Bases: Aldergrove, Newtownards, Long Kesh, Maghaberry, Nutts Corner, Ballyhalbert and Clifton

237 (Rhodesia) Sqn, *Primun agmen in caelo (The vanguard is in the sky)*
A/c: Mk I, November 1940 to November 1941; Mk II, November 1940 to November 1941
Bases: Gordons Tree, Blackdown, Agordat, Barentu, Agordat, Umritsar, Asmara, Waidi Halfa, Kufra, Kasfareet, 'Y' LG, LG 10 and LG75

239 Sqn, *Exploramus (We seek out)*
A/c: Mk II, September 1940 to May 1941; Mk III, April 1941 to January 1942
Code: HB
Bases: Hatfield, Gatwick, Cambridge, Weston Zoyland, Netheravon and Kidlington

241 Sqn, *Find and forewarn*
A/c: Mk II, September 1940 to December 1940; Mk III, December 1940 to May 1942
Code: RZ
Bases: Longman, Bury St Edmunds, Bottisham, Snailwell, Macmerry, Henlow and Docking

267 Sqn, *Sine mora (Without delay)*
A/c: Mk I, January 1941 to June 1942; Mk II, January 1941 to June 1942
Code: KW
Base: Heliopolis

268 Sqn, *Adjidaumo (Tail in the air)*
A/c: Mk II, September 1940 to April 1941; Mk III, February 1941 to March 1942
Code: NM
Bases: Bury St Edmunds, Cambridge, Snailwell, Ipswich, West Raynham, Barton Bendish, Penshurst, Twinwood Farm, Weston Zoyland, Docking and Ibsley

275 Sqn, *Non interibunt (They shall not perish)*
A/c: Mk III, October 1941 to September 1943
Code: PV
Bases: Valley, Andreas and Eglinton

276 Sqn, *Retrieve*
A/c: Mk IIIA, October 1941 to May 1943
Code: AQ
Bases: Harrowbeer, Roborough, Portreath, Warmwell, Perranporth and Fairwood Common

277 Sqn, *Quaerendo servamus (We save by seeking)*
A/c: Mk III, December 1941 to June 1944
Code: BA
Bases: Stapleford Tawney, Martlesham Heath, Hawkinge, Shoreham, Gravesend, Warmwell and Hurn

278 Sqn, *Ex mare ad referiendum (From out of the sea to strike again)*
A/c: Mk IIIA, October 1941 to February 1943
Code: MY
Bases: Matlaske, North Coates, Coltishall, Woolsington, Acklington, Hutton Cranswick, Ayr, Drem, Castletown, Peterhead and Sumburgh

285 Sqn, *Respice finem (Consider the end)*
A/c: Mk III, December 1941 to June 1942
Code: VG
Base: Wrexham

287 Sqn, *C'est en forgeant (Practice makes perfect)*
A/c: Mk III, November 1941 to April 1942
Code: KZ
Bases: Croydon, Debden, Hornchurch, Merston, Martlesham Heath, Fairlop, Biggin Hill, Northolt, Ipswich, Ford, Honiley, Hunsdon, Southend and Farnborough

288 Sqn, *Honour through deeds*
A/c: Mk II, November 1941 to March 1942; Mk III, November 1941 to March 1942
Code: RP
Bases: Digby, Church Fenton and Duxford

289 Sqn
A/c: Mk III, November 1941 to March 1942
Code: YE
Base: Kirknewton

309 (Ziema Czerwienska) Sqn
A/c: Mk III, November 1940 to May 1941; Mk IIIA, May 1941 to July 1942
Codes: AR and ZR
Bases: Abbotsinch, Renfrew, Perth/Scone, Dunino, Gatwick, Longman and Findo Gask

357 Sqn, *Mortem hostibus (We bring death to the enemy)*
A/c: Mk IIIA, March 1945 to November 1945
Bases: Jessore, Meiktila, Mingaladon and Don Muang

400 (City of Toronto) Sqn, *Percussuri vigiles (On watch to strike)*
A/c: Mk III, March 1941 to December 1941
Code: SP
Bases: Odiham, Redhill, Gatwick, Bottisham and Weston Zoyland

414 (Sarnia Imperials) Sqn, *Totis Viribis (With all our might)*
A/c: Mk III, August 1941 to June 1942
Code: RU
Base: Croydon

510 Sqn
A/c: Mk I, October 1942 to January 1943
Base: Hendon

516 Sqn
A/c: Mk II, April 1943 to December 1943
Base: Dundonald

598 Sqn
A/c: Mk IIIA, December 1943 to January 1944
Bases: Peterhead, Longman, Skaebrae, Sumburgh, Montrose and Turnhouse

613 (City of Manchester) Sqn, *Semper parati (Always ready)*
A/c: Mk II, April 1940 to January 1941; Mk IIIA, January 1941 to September 1942
Codes: ZR and SY
Bases: Odiham, Netherthorpe, Firbeck, Clifton, Sutton Bridge, Doncaster, Martlesham Heath, Doncaster, Weston Zoyland, Twinwood Farm and Ouston

614 (County of Glamorgan) Sqn, *Codaf I geislo (I rise to search)*
A/c: Mk II, July 1939 to July 1941; Mk III, April 1941 to January 1942
Codes: YX and LJ
Bases: Pengam Moors, Odiham, Weston Zoyland, Grangemouth, Evanton, Montrose, Longman, Dumfries, Tangmere, Macmerry, Westhampnett, Dalcross, Elgin, Clifton, West Raynham and Thruxton

695 Sqn, *We exercise their arms*
A/c: Mk I, December 1943 to January 1944; Mk II, December 1943 to January 1944
Code: 4M
Base: Bircham Newton

RAF second-line units
Aden Communication Flight; 2 (O)AFU; 3 (O)AFU (TT); 4 (O)AFU; 9 (O)AFU; 1 AAS; AFEE; 21 AD; 1 AGS; 2 AGS; 3 AGS; 4 AGS; 7 AGS; 8 AGS; 9 AGS; 10 AGS; 13 AGS; 1 AOS; 2 AOS; 4 AOS; 5 AOS; ASR Flts (UK) (10 Gp – 1, 2, 3 and 4 Flts; 11 Gp – 5, 6, 7 and 8 Flts; 12 Gp – 9 and 10 Flts); Air Transport Auxiliary (Training) Ferry Pool; 1 Anti-Aircraft Calibration Flt; 'A' Flt 1 AACU; 'B' Flt 1 AACU; 'D' Flt

1 AACU; 'F' Flt 1 AACU; 'H'; Flt 1 AACU; 'M' Flt 1 AACU; 'O' Flt 1 AACU; 'P' Flt 1 AACU; 6 AACU; 7 AACU; 8 AACU; 22 AACU; 1 AACU (IAF); 3 AACU (IAF); 1 Anti-Aircraft Practice Camp, Locking; 2 AAPC, Langham; 3 AAPC, Felixstowe (Ipswich); 4 AAPC, Towyn; 6 AAPC, Acklington; 8 AAPC, Montrose; 1, 2, 3, 4, 11, 16 and 17 APC; 3 Armament Training Camp; Army Co-operation Command Communication Flt; Army Co-operation Pool; (No.1) School of Army Co-operation; No.2 School of Army Co-operation; Bengal Communication Flt; 7 B&GS; 31 B&GS, Canada; Central Gunnery School; Central Landing Establishment; Central Navigation School; 3 Civil Maintenance Unit; 1 Combat Training Wing; 1333 and 1653 CU; 1414 Flt; 416 (Army Co-operation) Flt; 419 (Special Duties) Flt; 1416 (Reconnaissance) Flt; 1419 (Special Duties) Flt; 1424 (Air Observation Post) Flt; 1433 Flt; 1441 (Combined Operations Development) Flt; 1447 Flt; 1480 (Anti-Aircraft Co-operation) Flt; 1481, 1482, 1483, 1484, 1485, 1486, 1487, 1488, 1489,1490, 1491, 1492, 1493, 1494, 1495, 1496, 1497, 1498 and 1500 (Target-Towing) Flt; 4 and 1504 BATF (Beam Approach Training Flight); 1568 Meteorological Flt; 1601, 1625, 1626, 1627, 1628, 1630, 1631, 1632, 1633 and 1634 Anti-Aircraft Co-operation) Flt; Flying Training Command Communication Flt; 10 Flying Training School; 31 Service Flying Training School, Canada; Detachement Du Cameroun (D.A.C.); Detachement Du Moyen Congo Et Du Gabon; Detachement Permanent Des Forces Aeriennesdu Tchad (D.A.T.); 3 School of General Reconnaissance; 5 Glider Training School; 1 Ground Defence Gunners School; 9 Gp Anti-Aircraft Co-operation Flt; 10 Gp AACF; 11 Gp AACF; 12 Gp AACF; 13 Gp AACF; 1 Gp Communication Flight; 2 Gp CF; 3 Gp CF; 4 Gp CF; 5 Gp CF; 8 Gp CF; 9 Gp CF; 14 Gp CF; 15 Gp CF; 16 Gp CF; 18 Gp CF; 19 Gp CF; 82 Gp CF; 201 Gp CF; 204 Gp CF; 221 Gp CF; 1 Gp Target Towing Flt; 2 Gp TTF; 3 Gp TTF; 4 Gp TTF; 5 Gp TTF; 6 Gp TTF; 9 Gp TTF; 10 Gp TTF; 11 Gp TTF; 12 Gp TTF; 13 Gp TTF; 14 Gp TTF; 82 Gp TTF; 5 Gp Training Flt; Air Headquarters India Communication Unit; Communication Flt, Khartoum; Air HQ Levant Communication Flt; Communication Flt, Lydda; The Lysander Flt; 1 (Coastal) Operational Training Unit; 2 (Coastal) OTU; 3 (Coastal) OTU; 4 (Coastal) OTU; 5, 6 and 7 OTU; 8 (Coastal) OTU; 9 (Coastal)OTU; 10, 11, 12, 13, 14, 15, 16, 18, 19, 20, 21, 22, 23, 24, 25, 26, 27, 28, 29, 30, 31, 32, 34, 36, 41, 42, 43, 51, 53, 54, 55, 56, 58, 59, 60 and 61 OTU; 70 (Middle East) OTU; 71, 74 and 81 OTU; 102 (Glider) OTU; 132 (Coastal) OTU; 151 (Fighter) OTU; 1 OTU (India); 1 RAF Regiment School; 3 RAF Regiment School; Special Duty Flt; Station Flights – Aldergrove, Andover, Asansol, Beaulieu, Boscombe Down, Bottisham, Catfoss, Catterick, Coltishall, Coningsby, Driffield, Dundonald, Eastchurch, Fairwood Common, Gibraltar, Goxhill, Hawkinge, Hutton Cranswick, Inverness, Kaldadames, Kenley, Lydda, Manston, Mildenhall, Netheravon, Newmarket, Northolt, Odiham, Old Sarum, Pembrey, Perranporth, Portreath, Reykjavik, Ringway, Roborough, Salmesbury, Talbenny, Tangmere, Warmwell, Weston Zoyland, West Raynham, White Waltham and Wyton; 1 Torpedo Training Unit; 2 TTU; Transport & Communication Flt; West Africa Communication Sqn; Communication Flt, Air Headquarters Western Desert/Communication Unit, Western Desert; 239 Wing and 'D' Flt.

Fleet Air Arm

754 Sqn
A/c: Mk IIIA, June 1941 to March 1944
Code: W5
Base: Arbroath

755 Sqn
A/c: TT Mk III, July 1941 to October 1944; TT Mk IIIA, July 1941 to October 1944
Code: W6
Base: Worthy Down

757 Sqn
A/c: Mk III, April 1942 to December 1942
Code: X6
Base: Worthy Down

Foreign Air Force service
Royal Australian Air Force
3 Sqn, *Operta Aperta (Secrets Revealed)*
A/c: Mk II, August 1940 to January 1941

451 Sqn, *Into the midst from above*
A/c: Mk I and II, 1941 to 1942
Code: BQ
Bases: Kasfareet, Aboukir, Qasaba, LG 75, LG 132, LG 128, LG 145, LG 146, El Gubbi, LG 131, LG 148, Sid Azeiz, Heliopolis, Rayak and Estabel

Burma Volunteer Air Force
A/c: Mk II, March 1942 to December 1942
Bases: Mingaladon, Kyaikto, Syriam, Megui, Pokpyin and Lekokon

Finnish Air Force
12 Sqn (LLv.12), 14 Sqn (LLv.14), 16 Sqn (LLv.16) and 21 Sqn (HleLv.21)
A/c: All Mk II
Bases: Hirvas (12 Sqn), Solomanni (16 Sqn)

Free French Air Force (Forces Aériennes Françaises Libres)
'Bretagne' Groupe, 'Artois' Groupe and the Free French Flying School
A/c: Mk II

Irish Air Corps
1st Fighter Sqn
A/c: Mk II, July 1939 to April 1947
Codes: 61-66
Base: Baldonnel

Portuguese Air Force
BA3 and 361 Grup de Reconhecimento e Informacao
A/c: Mk IIIA

Turkish Air Force
A/c: Mk II
Base: Yesilkoy

United States Army Air Force
330th BS, 457th BS; 340th BS; 496th FTG; 2025th GF and 2031st GF
A/c: Mk IIIA and Mk IIIA TT

Westland Lysander Mk III, T1613, of 2 Squadron alongside a Mustang Mk I, also of 2 Squadron, at Sawbridgeworth in May 1942. While the Lysander was designed for the army co-operation role, the Mustang was designed as a fighter, but it proved to be particularly adept at the task, the Allison-powered variants excelling in the role. (*Aeroplane*)

A trio of Bristol Perseus XII-powered Lysander Mk Is are put through their paces for the camera in 1938. Very few Lysander Mk Is were serving with operational squadrons at the outbreak of World War Two, with the exception of 16 Squadron, which was re-equipped with the mark between May and September 1940. (*Aeroplane*)

The Lysander was one of three British-designed aircraft that formed the foundations of the modern RCAF; the other two being the Blenheim (Bolingbroke) and the Hurricane. Note the 'Serviceable' label on the inside of the cockpit canopy is for the benefit of the pilot and not the viewer. (Via Martyn Chorlton)

Other books you might like:

Historic Military Aircraft Series, Vol. 17

Historic Military Aircraft Series, Vol. 16

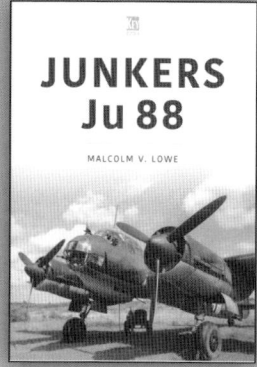

Historic Military Aircraft Series, Vol. 15

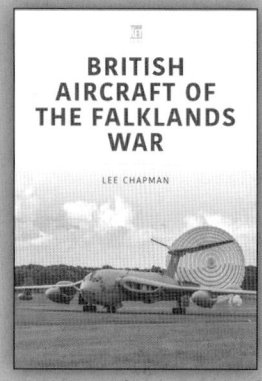

Historic Military Aircraft Series, Vol. 13

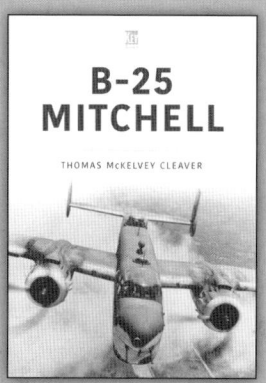

Historic Military Aircraft Series, Vol. 12

Historic Military Aircraft Series, Vol. 11

For our full range of titles please visit:
shop.keypublishing.com/books